Life is not a picnic.

Says who?

Picnic in Pisticci

by Tina Marie Theresa
D'Alessandro Powell

Copyright © 2012 by Big Fat Pen Publishing Inc.
Text copyright © 2012 by Tina Powell
Original photos and illustrations copyright © 2012 by Big Fat Pen Publishing Inc.

All rights reserved. No part of this book may be used, reproduced, transmitted in any form or by any means, electronic, mechanical, recording, or otherwise, or stored in a retrieval system, without prior written permission of the publisher, Big Fat Pen Publishing Inc.
www.bigfatpen.com

First Edition

Library and Archives Canada Cataloguing in Publication

Powell, Tina, 1962-
Picnic in Pisticci : my search for the perfect picnic / Tina Marie Theresa D'Alessandro Powell.

Includes bibliographical references.
Includes some text in Italian.
ISBN 978-0-9737799-6-7

1. Picnics. 2. Powell, Tina, 1962-. I. Title.

GT2955.P69 2011   642'.3   C2011-900743-6

Cover art by Farida Zaman
Design by MAD marketing+design
Editing by Susan Petersiel Berg
Permissions by Dania Sheldon
Translation by SB Language Services
Printed in Canada

Great care has been taken to locate the owners of all material held under copyright in this book and to gain permission for republication. Big Fat Pen Publishing Inc. apologizes for any errors that may have occurred in the permissions process and will rectify any incorrect references or credits in subsequent editions. If you have any inquiries regarding the material included in this book, please contact Big Fat Pen Publishing Inc.
Pages 97 to 101 are considered an extension of the copyright page.

In loving memory of John and Camilla D'Alessandro, my grandparents, from Pisticci, Italy.

Me as a baby with my grandparents and big sister.

"Superbly crafted and genuinely written, *Picnic in Pisticci* proves the written power of a wonderfully talented raconteur. Tina Powell's heartfelt story and recollections engage, delight, and bring a warm feeling to your soul…"
– Howard Breen, Author, *A page from a CEO's Diary* and *The Toothpick Factory*

"No picnic is perfect, which is why they are so important; each holds the potential for discovery – and in the hands of author Tina Powell, any picnic is a platform for laughter, for truthtelling, and for the love of place. Her writing sparks as many 'oh nos' as it does the envy of 'I want to be there.' Everything fits like a smooth blanket on bumpy grass, pinned in the corners by mugs of root beer and bowls of salad. I could taste this book as I read it."
– Rick Antonson, Author / President and CEO of Tourism Vancouver

I could taste this

"A delightful romp through the joys of picnics; written with humour, inspiration, and a keen sense of what's really important in life. One of those books that will be passed along from friend to friend; a creative and original gem that will be sure to put a smile on your face!"
– Evaleen Jaager Roy, Author, *Four Chefs One Garden*

"*Picnic in Pisticci* is a wonderfully reflective tale of picnics that have punctuated the ebb and flow of Tina Powell's life – from her first to her most recent, when three generations gathered in their ancestral town of Pisticci, Italy. With each experience a larger, deeper story unfolds."
– Andrea Disario, Marketing Communications Executive

"Life, like picnics, isn't about perfection. It is about grabbing those moments that matter and sharing them with the people you love. Tina, by sharing the stories of the picnics of her life, evokes the feelings and memories that many of us have experienced."
– Julia Hanna, Owner, Ristorante Julia and Ritorno / Founder, Kids Culinary Community

"I loved this book ... it took me back in time to when I looked forward to the little things that meant so much ... when something so simple, like a picnic or family get-together, held so much possibility. *Picnic in Pisticci* will remind you of the important things in life, 'friends, family, play, and peace... '"
– Tammy Preast, Entrepreneur, Ask A Woman Enterprises Ltd.

"Tina Powell's *Picnic in Pisticci* highlights the stolen moments of getting away from the constraints of the daily business of life to share a potluck meal and enjoy spontaneous moments of joy and love with family and friends."
– Jo Altilia, Founding Executive Director, Literature for Life

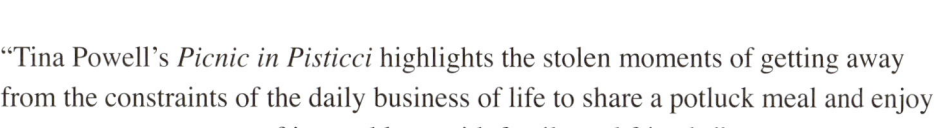

book as I read it...

"Tina Powell has surprised us with this new, uplifting, and humorous story. In sharing personal memoirs, Tina inspires us to create our own memories and shows us that even though we may strive for perfection, it is in the planning, sharing, and doing that life's best moments can happen – perfect or not."
– Suzy Johnston, Artists' Representative

"By mapping her personal journey through the picnics of life, Tina Powell creates a fantastic trip down memory lane for any picnic lover, including me! Now, where is my pic-a-nic basket?"
– Angela Crocker, TheBookBroads.com

"It warn't anything but a Sunday-school picnic, and only a primer class at that. We busted it up, and chased the children up the hollow; but we never got anything but some doughnuts and jam, though Ben Rogers got a rag doll, and Joe Harper got a hymn-book and a tract; and then the teacher charged in, and made us drop everything and cut."

– *THE ADVENTURES OF HUCKLEBERRY FINN*, Mark Twain

CONTENTS

Foreword by Massimo Capra   12

CHAPTER 1	My First Picnic	14
CHAPTER 2	Fun with Jim and Jane	20
CHAPTER 3	Looking for Love	24
CHAPTER 4	A Grand Beginning	30
CHAPTER 5	All I Really Need	36
CHAPTER 6	In Good Company	40
CHAPTER 7	Feeling Red, White ... and Red	46
CHAPTER 8	A Picnic Revelation	52
CHAPTER 9	Home Is Where the Picnic Is	58
CHAPTER 10	Our Picnic in Pisticci	64

Acknowledgements   96
Credits   97

Massimo Capra
Celebrity Chef,
Cookbook Author, and
Executive Chef Co-Owner
of Mistura Restaurant
and Sopra Lounge
in Toronto, Canada

Over the years, I have enjoyed many picnics with my family. It is a tradition to gather young and old, drive some distance to a park, and spend the day eating, drinking, and playing outdoor games. Having a picnic is a great way to relax and enjoy the day. It is an opportunity to unplug from modern life and get in touch with close ones. I can still remember my first picnic ... it was a warm summer day back in 1968 when I first experienced a modern picnic ... and I will never forget the adventure.

I was only eight years old when my cousins, Fausto and Bruna, purchased a new car: a brand, spanking new Fiat 850, baby blue of course, the latest release from the popular car company. That day, over dinner, the idea of going on a picnic in the Tuscan hills was hatched and the itinerary was drawn; we would visit Florence and its churches, of course, and then we would go to the countryside, stop in a vineyard to buy fresh fruit, and enjoy a lunch al fresco.

My mother worked for two days preparing all the food. On the morning of the big trip, I was so excited that I awoke at 4 a.m. and was ready to go. My mother finished making the fresh salads and packed them into bowls wrapped with cloths and elastic bands to prevent the salads from getting dirty. The boneless stuffed chicken was ready and hot, along with the lasagna and the pork cutlets Milanese. Everything was placed carefully into a couple of

baskets to separate hot from cold. My father was in charge of the beverages, so he packed some bottles of homemade wine and we were ready to go.

The five of us squeezed into that small car and we left my hometown at 6 a.m. sharp. We arrived in Florence by 9 a.m., visited the important landmarks, and at 1 p.m. we left the city centre to find a place to eat. It wasn't long before we stopped at a friendly farmhouse and asked permission to set up our picnic by the vines. The kind farmer was happy to say yes and even gave us some Tuscan bread to go with our food. He also suggested that we trade our wine for some of his. I remember my father and cousins were very happy with the exchange.

The memory of eating al fresco with my family will never fade away ... the long drive in a new car ... the excitement of visiting a beautiful city ... and the freedom of eating in the shade of a vineyard were all so stimulating. The food, of course, was exquisite ... and if I close my eyes, I can still taste it.

Although it has been many years since I thought about that delectable picnic in Tuscany, the memories came flooding back thanks to author Tina Powell. I hope *Picnic in Pisticci* helps you to savour your own picnic memories and encourages you to create some new ones with family and friends.

Buon appetito!

My First Picnic

What to pack:

fried chicken

chocolate brownies

coleslaw

watermelon

root beer

Picnics promise happiness

As far as I am concerned, this was my first picnic. I have been told that there were others before it, but I don't recall them. I have only heard stories and seen photographs. I remember this picnic in particular because it's the picnic that almost wasn't.

Memories are a lot like dreams. Fleeting. Distant. Beyond reach. No pursing of lips, closing of eyes, or furrowing of brows will help in the recollection process. Fragments float in and out of your consciousness. The details dissolve before your eyes and you can't help but wonder, "Did it really happen?" For me, extreme emotion cements a memory. I may struggle with dates, times, places, faces, and names; but feelings I never forget. In the case of this picnic, I was feeling utter despair.

I was 10 years old. My family and I were planning to go on a picnic with my Uncle Tony, Aunt Gloria, and younger cousins, Paul and Joanne. Although I can't be certain, I am pretty sure the picnic was my uncle's idea. To know my father is to know that the words, "Let's go on a picnic with my brother and his family!" wouldn't readily pop out of his mouth. It's not that he didn't love his brother. He did, intensely. It's just that my father's idea of quality family time was to spend it with my mom, my sisters, and me – an intimate affair, by invitation only. He wasn't a big fan of extended family reunions, neighbourhood block parties, or horror of all horrors, church potluck suppers.

– *THE BEARS' PICNIC*,
Stan Berenstain and Jan Berenstain

My Mom's Potato Salad

6 medium sized potatoes
4 green onions, thinly sliced
4 stalks of celery, thinly sliced
3/4 cup mayonnaise
2 Tbsp milk
1 tsp sugar
1/2 tsp garlic powder
4 hard-boiled eggs
paprika

Boil unpeeled potatoes in salted water until tender. Remove from heat and when cool to touch, remove potato skins by hand. Dice potatoes into bite-sized cubes and place in a large bowl. Add sliced onions and celery. In a small bowl, mix 1/2 cup of the mayonnaise with milk, sugar, and garlic powder. Add mayonnaise mixture to potatoes and mix gently. Add remaining 1/4 cup of mayonnaise and mix again. Slice hard-boiled eggs and garnish top of salad with egg slices. Sprinkle lightly with paprika. Cover and refrigerate overnight.

Tina's Tip: Sprinkle with bacon bits and shredded cheddar before serving.

Makes 4 to 6 servings.

66 sleeps until our picnic in Pisticci.
Today's Forecast:
More sun than clouds.
Temperature of 24°C.
30% chance of precipitation.

At the time, I didn't get it. Who doesn't love a good party? But now I think I understand. I believe my father was tired of constantly having to perform. As a businessman and an entrepreneur, he spent much of his time with customers, selling, servicing, and shmoozing. The hours were long and the stakes were high. He always had to be "up" or "on." It must have been exhausting. Maybe, at home with his family, my dad could just "be." He could be himself … and he could be with us.

But at 10 years old, it's all about "the more the merrier" and you couldn't find anyone merrier than my Uncle Tony. The words of Clement Clarke Moore best capture my Uncle Tony: "He had a broad face and a little round belly, that shook, when he laughed, like a bowlful of jelly. He was chubby and plump, a right jolly old elf, and I laughed when I saw him, in spite of myself." To me, Uncle Tony was Santa Claus. Not just because of his generosity and girth, but because he had a *joie de vivre* that was both foreign and intoxicating to me. He was always ready for a good time, a good laugh, or a good meal.

My Uncle Tony had the best of everything. He had the coolest car ever – a station wagon. His home had central air conditioning *and* a swimming pool. The soda pop at his house came in individual cans, not big bottles, and he used special plastic bags for his kitchen garbage; no leaky, brown, paper grocery bags for him! He always served the best food: takeout Chinese,

Kentucky Fried Chicken, and not just potato chips, but dip, too ... and the *pièce de résistance*, Bugles. I can still remember biting off the pointy end and pretending to blow a bugle reveille. Plus, every year he took my aunt and cousins to the most spectacular place in the whole world – Disney World! Even the Brady Bunch kids had never been to Disney! Hawaii and the Grand Canyon, sure, but never Disney.

You can imagine the all-encompassing joy I felt when I found out that we were going on a picnic to Niagara Falls with my Uncle Tony. I counted down the sleeps until the glorious day. I imagined the delicious food my mother would surely pack – all my favourites: tuna sandwiches, potato salad, homemade pizza, chocolate brownies, watermelon, and root beer. I wondered if Uncle Tony and Aunt Gloria would grant me access to their picnic basket: fried chicken, hoagie sandwiches, Italian sausage, Ziggy's coleslaw and macaroni salads, doughnuts, and candy. As a child – ok, make that all my life – I have had a hard time resisting great food.

Finally, the day was almost upon us. One more sleep to go. And then the unthinkable happened. One of us got sick. I don't recall who it was. Maybe it was my sister Cam. Or my sister Michelle. Maybe it was me. One of us got a terrible, horrible, nose-honking, mucus-making, you-can-call-me-Sneezy, temperature-rising, get-to-bed, NO-PICNIC-FOR-YOU cold. My dad called my Uncle Tony and cancelled the picnic.

"Picnic – a casual, friendly meal taken on a day trip, eaten outdoors, usually in summer, from the French *piquer*, meaning 'to pick at food,' and *nique*, meaning 'something small or inconsequential.' Originally, 'picnic' referred to an informal meal in which everyone paid their share or brought their own dish."

– *THE FOOD ENCYCLOPEDIA*

(L to R) Me and my sister Cam at our family picnic in Niagara Falls, Canada.

(L to R) My sister Michelle and cousin Joanne happily watch their toy windmills spin with the breeze from Niagara Falls.

"I don't feel that I could endure the disappointment if anything happened to prevent me from getting to the picnic. I suppose I'd live through it, but I'm certain it would be a lifelong sorrow."

– *ANNE OF GREEN GABLES,*
L.M. Montgomery

There were tears. There was sobbing. There was pleading and begging. "Please, please don't cancel the picnic! It's just a little cold. We have to go. Pleeeeease, can we go?" Not surprisingly, my parents didn't understand my extreme reaction. Why did this picnic mean so much to me? Did I have some inexplicable, psychological need to see a natural wonder of the world? Was the prospect of not spending the entire day with my Uncle Tony and his family that unbearable? Did I have a bizarre addiction to fried chicken and watermelon? No, the answers did not lie here.

Although I couldn't articulate it then, I have come to realize that picnics, to me, represent perfection. Perfect weather. Perfect food. Perfect fun. Perfect family. For one day my family would be perfect, just like the happy, fictional families I saw on television. We would be the Waltons, or the Partridges, or the Bradys. I could be Elizabeth Walton, or Laurie Partridge, or Jan Brady (my older sister Cam always got to play Marcia). We would find the perfect picnic spot, unpack our wicker basket, spread out a red-and-white checkered tablecloth, and have a delectable feast. We would fly kites, kick soccer balls, and play board games. We would laugh, and sing, and talk. Yes, for just one day we would be perfectly happy.

The truth is my family wasn't always happy. We had our share of good times and we had our share of challenging times. We had our moments of glory and our moments of failure.

We shared laughter and we shed tears. I understand now, of course, that my family was no different from any other family. But as a little girl, I thought something was wrong with us. I thought we were the only ones who were not happy all the time. I thought that by going on this picnic, we would somehow be perfect, too.

We would be the Waltons...

At the age of 10, I knew the promise of happiness would elude us unless I did something drastic. I couldn't put it into words. I could, though, like every child, put on an Oscar-worthy performance. I stopped the begging. I stopped the pleading. I stopped the nagging. I didn't say a word. I just sat there. My lips quivered. My saucer eyes brimmed with tears. My body shuddered when I sighed. And I waited.

At around 11 o'clock that evening (these things take time) my dad called my Uncle Tony and said, "I've got some pretty sad faces around here. How would you feel about resurrecting the picnic?" Pretty good, apparently, because we did go on that picnic and it was everything I had hoped it would be. I still remember standing by the Falls with my family, feeling the spray of the mist on my face, and thinking all was right in my world.

Surely a trip to Disney wouldn't be far in my future!

Whatever may have been its origin, today the picnic is a predominately British institution. Maybe the lamentably low standard of English cooking has something to do with the matter. Abroad the traveller may be sure of good food and good drink in the smallest village inn, but in England he may well prefer to pack a picnic meal and eat in the open air, regardless of the weather, rather than face the gastronomic rigours of the British hotel.

– *ENGLISH PICNICS*, Georgina Battiscombe

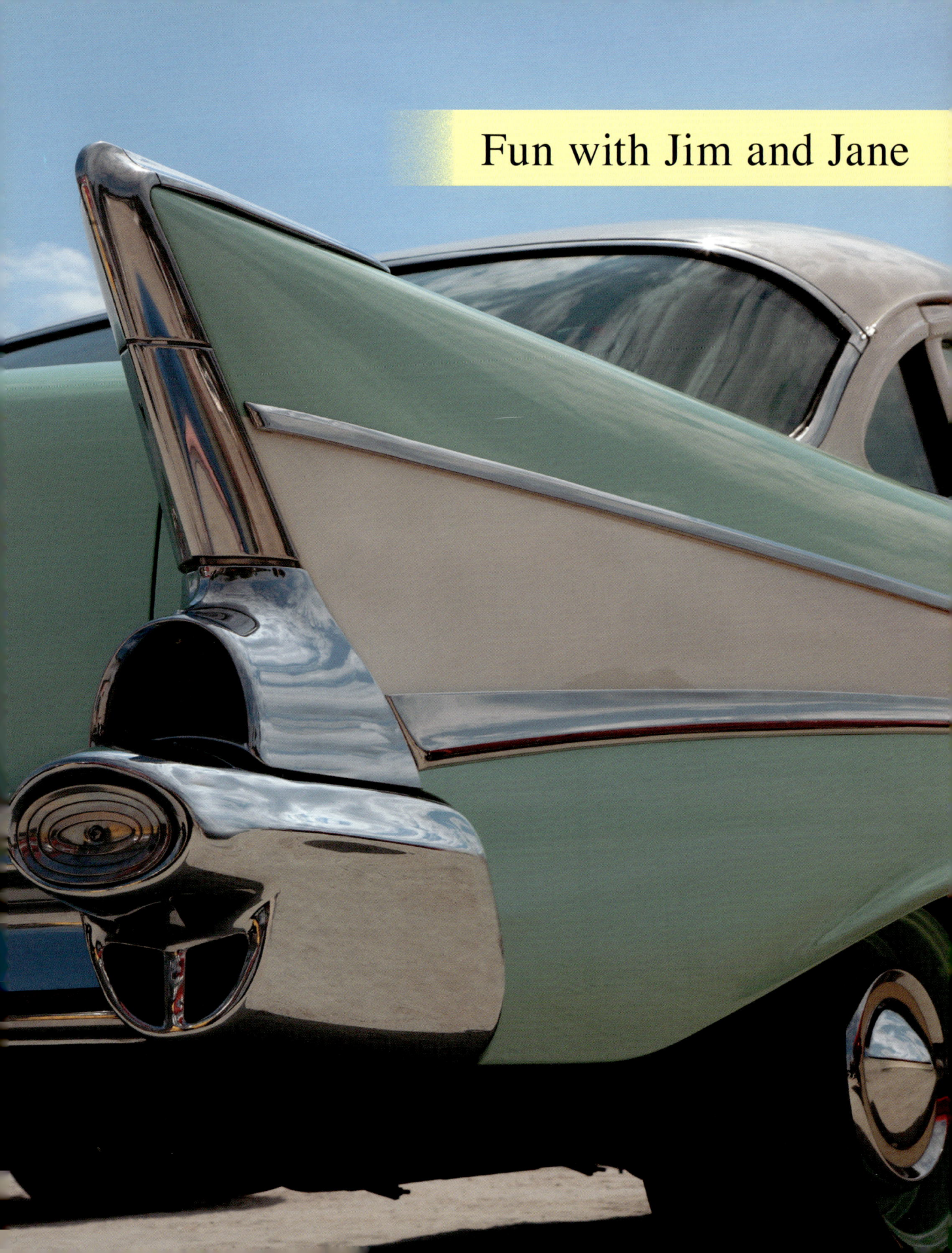
Fun with Jim and Jane

Picnics promise memories

My parents' names are Jim and Jane. I always thought it had a nice ring to it. Kind of like Antony and Cleopatra, Samson and Delilah, Lucy and Ricky, and Joanie and Chachi. Although my parents are no longer a couple, we did have our share of "Happy Days" as a family. We still laugh about family vacation mishaps, Halloween costumes that backfired, and home renovations that today would make a wildly entertaining reality TV show: Survivor, the Extreme Home Makeover Edition.

Prior to my memorable "first" picnic in Niagara Falls, there was another family picnic. We'll have to take Jim and Jane's word that it actually occurred because I was too young to remember it. By the sound of it, I'd be in therapy today if I did.

Some could argue that this forgettable picnic did not even qualify as a picnic. Take the location, for starters – a grassy berm at the off-ramp of a busy highway. This is hardly an ideal picnic setting. Not only is it an incredibly dangerous place to throw a football or play tag, it is about as picturesque as a city dump or a field with power lines overhead. Furthermore, grassy berms along busy highways are popular locations to relieve full bladders and queasy stomachs. This may explain the biblical number of flies

" 'Cookies, cookies,' said Sally. 'See the three big cookies. One for Dick and one for Jane. One for me and one for Spot.' "

– *THE NEW WE COME AND GO*, William S. Gray

"One of the most successful picnics I ever had was in a parking lot on the New Jersey Turnpike, where four of us sat looking out at trees, ignored trucks and cars, and enjoyed champagne, filet of beef, sandwiches, salad, cheese, and fruit."

– "The Art of Picnicking" in THE ARMCHAIR JAMES BEARD, James Beard

My family and I once picnicked at this busy freeway off-ramp.

my mother vividly recalls, or why the cows in the neighbouring farmer's field sauntered over for a closer look.

To make matters worse, the food for this picnic was all wrong. There were no sandwiches, no salads, no lemonade, no watermelon. Instead, we had hotdogs and French fries purchased at the gas-station snack bar, also located at this idyllic highway off-ramp.

Don't get me wrong. I love a good ballpark frank smothered in mustard and sauerkraut, and a trip to the beach at Grand Bend isn't complete without an order of Denny's fries and gravy. What's more, there is absolutely nothing wrong with picnicking at the side of the road while *heading* to another destination.

But this picnic outing was not advertised that way. Family members, whose names I have concealed out of the goodness of my heart, enthusiastically invited my family on a "traditional family picnic." Jim and Jane were told to leave everything to these other well-meaning family members who would take care of the food, the location, and all the activities. The day was billed as a wonderful opportunity for our young families to bond.

Perhaps it was an innocent misunderstanding. Perhaps the original plan had to be abandoned because the children were acting up. (My mom does recall someone whining incessantly in the back seat, but she's certain it was an adult!) Or perhaps these people had no freaking idea what a picnic is supposed to be!

Apparently, my family and I ate our hotdogs and fries, in the scorching hot sun, as the flies buzzed around, and the cars zoomed past, and the cows watched, and then we went home, promising never again to fall prey to pesky picnic poseurs.

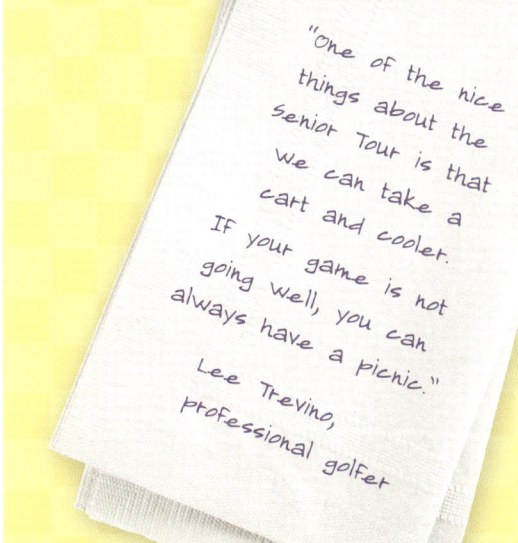

"One of the nice things about the Senior Tour is that we can take a cart and cooler. If your game is not going well, you can always have a picnic."

Lee Trevino, professional golfer

...and the cows watched

Not all family outings can be Hallmark moments. Some are really bad TV sitcoms. That's life. If you're really lucky, though, one day you'll look back on memories like these and laugh – just like Jim and Jane still do.

A Tasty Picnic Blanket

1 seedless watermelon
1 large seeded honeydew melon

Slice watermelon and honeydew into half-inch-thick square pieces of equal size. Arrange pieces on a platter to create a checkered picnic blanket. Garnish with a trail of chocolate-covered-raisin "ants."

Picnics promise innocence

I am not sure how I feel about my daughter, or for that matter my husband, reading about this next picnic. And it's downright scary to think about my parents reading it. Can a woman in her late forties be grounded?

I was about my daughter's age when this particular picnic occurred. As a parent, it's difficult to imagine your own children thinking, feeling, and doing the things that you did when you were their age. Perhaps it's naïveté on my part. Perhaps it's a built-in protection mechanism. Regardless, I am always guaranteed to get a good laugh from other parents of teens when I proclaim that there is no chance that my teenaged children have indulged in sex, drugs, or alcohol. Invariably, I look ridiculous and sputter defiantly, "But my children are different. I would know if they were into that." Right. Just like my mother knew the first time I drank alcohol.

Gulp!

But back to my picnic story. I was working at Robinson's Pharmacy, a small-town, one-cash-register, independent drugstore. I was the one and only part-time cashier. Most of our customers were senior citizens stopping by for a chat and to pick up their monthly prescriptions.

Little girls, this seems to say,
Never stop upon your way.
Never trust a stranger-friend;
No one knows how it will end.
As you're pretty, so be wise;
Wolves may lurk in every guise.
Handsome they may be, and kind,
Gay, or charming never mind!
Now, as then, 'tis simple truth
Sweetest tongue has sharpest tooth!

– Moral to *LITTLE RED RIDING HOOD*,
Charles Perrault,
as translated by S.R. Littlewood

On this particular summer day, there was a big rush at the front cash (three customers in line!). After ringing up and packaging the purchases of the first two customers, I looked up and I saw him. He had sandy blonde, windblown hair, mirrored sunglasses, and a deep, glistening tan that accentuated his bare muscular arms. He smiled

…I looked up and I saw him

"I've liked lots of people 'til I went on a picnic jaunt with them."

Bess Truman,
First Lady, United States

and exposed his perfect white teeth, and despite his reflective shades I could tell that he, too, was checking me out at the checkout. I looked down self-consciously. I was wearing a floral skirt of soft pastels: pink, yellow, blue, and green. My blouse was a silky, pale yellow and much to my Italian father's chagrin, it fit snugly in all the right (or wrong) places.

The consummate professional, I asked, "May I help you?" Imagine my surprise when he replied, "Hi, Tina." (I wasn't wearing a nametag.) He slowly removed his sunglasses. It was a boy I knew from school. A boy whom I had never noticed much, but who was now noticing my silky, pale yellow blouse.

His name was … hmmm. Author's dilemma. Should I reveal his name? What if someone from w Secondary School reads this book and

50 sleeps until our picnic in Pisticci.
Today's Forecast:
Sunny. Warm. Beautiful.
Temperature of 27°C.
0% chance of precipitation.

shares my picnic memory with him? What if my father, or for that matter my husband, reads this book and hunts him down in cold blood? I bet my dad and hubby would go together! Although you don't deserve it – you know who you are – I will spare you.

Mr. X and I chatted idly. The sparks between us were electric. He bought a package of chewing gum, leaned in close, and invited me to join him on a picnic lunch the following day. All afternoon I daydreamed about our romantic picnic rendezvous. The rest of the day floated by.

At noon the next day, he picked me up in his car and we drove speedily to the neighbourhood park. Unfortunately, I only had an hour for lunch. He marched ahead of me with a blanket he grabbed from the backseat and a brown paper bag. I hobbled across the grass field in my high-heeled sandals.

"This isn't so good," I thought.

The blanket was spread, the food was unwrapped, and I was encouraged to eat. Young Mr. X was not eating.

"This is really not good," I thought. It soon became wildly apparent that Mr. X was hungry for something other than a picnic lunch.

"This is soooooo bad," I thought.

Even back then, I knew that this was not how a picnic should be. Picnics are inherently good, and romantic picnics should be based upon

Rock Hudson and Dorothy Malone in *WRITTEN ON THE WIND*

Marylee: Oh, there's nothing like a picnic! And I brought everything but rain and ants. Oh, correction … everything but rain.

Screenplay by George Zuckerman, Courtesy of Universal Studios Licensing LLLP

"An open mind, it's been said, is the devil's picnic."

– *THE DEVIL'S PICNIC,*
Taras Grescoe

true love and affection. Picnics are a throwback to simpler, more innocent times; picnics are steeped in nostalgia and sentimentality. Picnics are so much more than a hurried, lust-filled lunch in a field on a blanket. Picnics are a celebration of all things that are good and right in this world: love, friendship, commitment, sharing, sincerity, and innocence.

I pushed Mr. X off of me and insisted on being driven back to work immediately.

After quiet reflection, I saw the situation for what it was and Mr. X for who he was. Thanks to this picnic, I was a little less naïve and a lot more careful.

My innocence isn't the only thing Mr. X couldn't take from me that day – he couldn't take away my romantic view of picnics, either. I would never give anyone that satisfaction.

Basic Devilled Eggs

12 hard-cooked eggs, peeled
1/4 cup mayonnaise
2 tsp Dijon mustard
salt, pinch to taste
ground pepper, pinch to taste

Cut eggs in half lengthwise. Remove yolks. With fork, mash yolks; add mayonnaise, Dijon mustard, salt, and pepper. Refill whites with yolk mixture.

Serve immediately or store, covered, in refrigerator. Use within 3 days.

Makes 24 devilled eggs.

To take devilled eggs to a picnic, put the cooked egg white halves in a plastic container and the devilled yolk filling in a plastic bag. Place both in the cooler. When you are ready to serve, cut off one corner of the plastic bag and pipe filling into the egg white halves. For distinctive devilled eggs, mix egg yolks with some chicken salad and stuff this mixture into the egg whites.

Courtesy of Egg Farmers of Canada

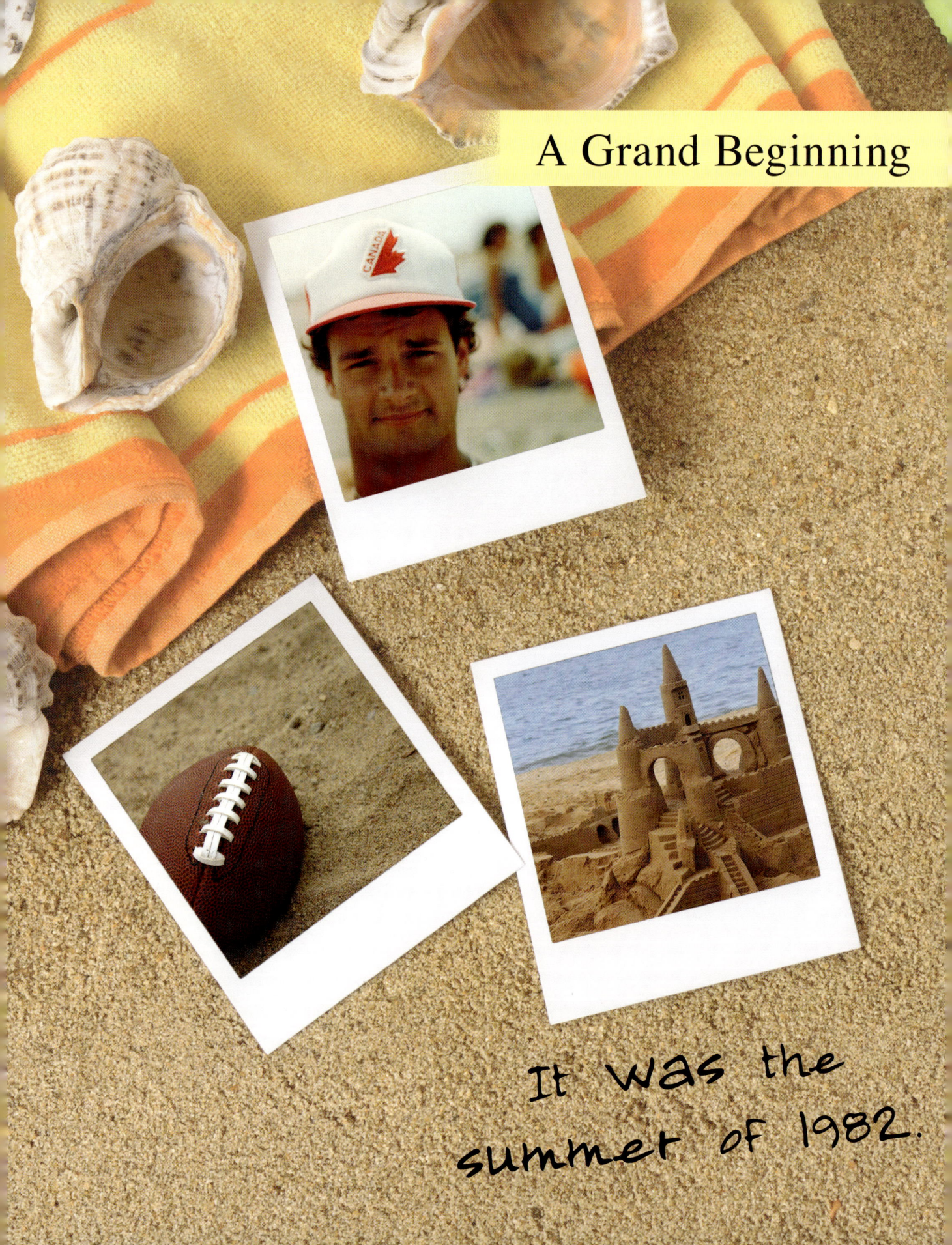

A Grand Beginning

It was the summer of 1982.

Picnics promise love

It is my belief that the world can be divided into two types of summer vacationers: beach people and lake people. Beach people delight in the slightest whiff of sunscreen, believe the four food groups are ice cream, French fries, barbecued hotdogs, and cream soda, and can't resist dipping their toes in a frothy, shoreline surf. These folks crave their daily uniform of flip-flops and bathing suits, and the screeching of seagulls is music to their ears.

Lake people, on the other hand, adore blackfly bites, mushy lake sediment between their toes, gasoline fumes from motor boats, and frequent visits from uninvited guests, such as raccoons and bears.

In case you have not guessed, I am a beach person to the core. You can imagine my relief when I found a kindred spirit in my husband, Randy. Married couples can survive opposing political views. They can settle religious differences through compromise and education. They can negotiate the great debate over skim or 2% milk. But a beach person and a lake person will never see beach ball to fishing rod. Regardless of political leanings, religious affiliations, and milk-fat preference, our mutual beachiness guaranteed that Randy and I were destined for something magical.

"My bounty is as boundless as the sea, / My love as deep; the more I give to thee, / The more I have, for both are infinite."

– *ROMEO AND JULIET*, William Shakespeare

Me on the first of many picnics at the beach in Grand Bend, Ontario.

38 sleeps until our picnic in Pisticci.
Today's Forecast:
Morning clouds.
Mild. Temperature of 25°C.
32% chance of precipitation.

A person's natural inclination to either side of the beach or lake debate is a matter of upbringing. From early childhood, my summer vacations were spent at my grandparents' cottage in Wasaga Beach on Georgian Bay. My definition of a blissful day was building sandcastles on the shore, reading Archie comic books on my beach towel, jumping the waves, and eating sandy French fries for lunch.

My husband spent his summers in Grand Bend, another popular beach community, a mere 150 miles away from Wasaga. Not only did Randy spend his summer days lying on the sand devouring comic books and French fries, he started his days in the exact same fashion as I did: a milk-and-cereal breakfast while watching children's TV favourites Mr. Dressup, Chez Hélène, and The Friendly Giant.

It therefore was with great delight that I accepted Randy's invitation to picnic with him in Grand Bend. It was the summer of 1982. He had just graduated from college and I was about to enter my final year. Into his gold Ford Fiesta we packed a cooler filled with sandwiches and cold drinks, a couple of well-worn beach blankets, a football, and a bottle of sunscreen – SPF 8, a rather extreme concept back then, when we'd only just stopped using baby oil in the sun.

Since we were looking at a drive of about two and a half hours through the communities of Milton, Kitchener, New Hamburg, Stratford, Exeter, and Dashwood, we decided to get an early start to the day. The sun was shining, the windows were down, and the radio was blaring. I looked across at Randy and I not only saw all that he meant to me at that moment – friendship, passion, adventure, and joy – I saw our future together. We were young. We were in love. And I'd never felt so alive.

I'd never felt so alive...

Unfortunately, I also had never felt so sick to my stomach. In all the excitement to pack the car and hit the road, I neglected to eat breakfast. Being a sufferer of motion sickness since childhood, I knew that an empty stomach and a long road trip were a lethal combination. Eager to keep the bloom of newfound love intact, I tried to ignore my growing nausea. With each passing mile, my complexion turned greener, my stomach did somersaults, and my smile faded.

"No, no, no," I thought. "I just can't get sick. It will ruin everything. Randy and I are beach people. Today is the day we are to consummate our beachiness. I'm supposed to toss a football, not toss my cookies!"

I turned toward the window and drank in the fresh country air. I could feel the stomach acid build in the back of my throat. I searched my purse in vain for a piece of gum or candy. The muscles in my

My husband and I still love Grand Bend – and each other – as much as ever.

On a picnic morning
without a warning
I looked at you
and somehow I knew
On a day for singing,
My heart went winging
A picnic grove
was our rendezvous

– PICNIC,
lyrics by George Duning
and Steve Allen

The Powell Family's Pasta Salad Recipe

4 cups elbow pasta
1 tin solid white tuna,
  packed in water, drained
2 stalks celery, sliced
8 Tbsp mayonnaise
salt and pepper to taste

Cook pasta in boiling water till tender (8 to 10 minutes). Drain pasta and add tuna, celery, and mayonnaise. Stir gently and season with salt and pepper. Cover and chill in refrigerator for several hours before serving.

face tightened uncontrollably. I wrapped my arms around my body, trying to hold my rolling stomach in one place. I gagged.

"Randy, pull over."

There's not much dignity in throwing up at the side of the road. With each heave from the cavern of my stomach, I saw my hopes of a perfect day picnicking at the beach slip away. There went my hopes of looking sexy in my black bathing suit. There went my hopes of splashing in the surf and stealing kisses in the waves. There went my hopes of strolling hand in hand along the shore, picking up shells, and writing our names in the sand.

From experience I knew it was over. This was not my first time vomiting in front of a prospective boyfriend. (I told my grade nine crush not to rock the Ferris wheel, but did he listen? No, he thought it was hilarious. That was until the inevitable happened. He wouldn't even look at me the next day at school.)

It was beyond over.

With that high-school memory burning in my mind but the acid no longer burning in my stomach, I eased back in the car. I was positive my roadside barf-o-rama would serve as the perfect excuse to turn the car around.

Silence.

I stole a sideways glance in Randy's direction. Was he actually smiling? I turned to face him. His eyes were full of love and kindness.

They were also twinkling with amusement. According to Randy, this was all kind of funny. And I wasn't repulsive, I was rather cute!

Our picnic date didn't end there. Once assured of my road-worthiness, we continued on our way. We baked in the sun, danced in the waves, shared our hopes and dreams over ice cream, and planned our future as we walked hand in hand along the shore.

Relationships are constantly put to the test. But if you begin with a strong foundation built on love, friendship, respect, trust, compassion, and above all, a mutual love of beaches (or lakes), you can thrive.

I'm not exactly sure why Randy was not repulsed by my motion sickness that day. Maybe love does conquer all. Maybe a bad bout of nausea is powerless against true love – or a great picnic. All I do know is that it's a good thing Randy thought I was a cute puker – he's seen me do it often enough over our more than 25 years of marriage.

My children, Mason and Kinsey, the next generation of beach cottagers, running along the shore at Grand Bend.

Our picnic date didn't end there…

All I Really Need

Picnics promise simplicity

I distinctly remember counting out the coins. As a young couple, Randy and I lived in a small basement apartment. We didn't know from one month to the next how we were going to manage our rent, our groceries, or gas for the car, let alone pay for a treat. We searched jacket pockets and old purses for loose change, celebrating each coin discovered. It was a chilly, overcast fall day and we were planning a picnic.

Our picnic blanket was neatly folded and we had assembled all of our favourite delicacies. We had romaine lettuce and Kraft Golden Caesar salad dressing. We had Tuc crackers and havarti cheese with caraway seeds. We had fresh green grapes and a bottle of Mateus wine. What more could a young, starving couple need? We had it all! And although we truly did not need a single thing more, there was one more thing we wanted. Which was why we were scrounging for change.

"Well, what do you think?" I asked. "Is it enough?"

Randy finished counting. "Oh, yeah. We're good." Randy always exudes such confidence.

"But what about…" I started.

"Well, if we don't have enough for that, there's no point," Randy replied. (He's such an all-or-nothing type of guy.) "We won't know for sure until we get there."

"Hey, Boo Boo, what do you think is in that pic-a-nic basket?"
– *THE YOGI BEAR SHOW*™

For the Sunday School Picnic at Stanley Park (Erin, Ontario), Maud recounts making a jelly roll, cherry pies, tarts, cookies, date loaf, sandwiches and lemonade. Quite a significant contribution from a busy author!

Homemade Pink Lemonade

1-1/2 cups red jelly
   (sour cherry, currant, or
   any other desired flavour)
1 cup sugar
2-1/2 cups lemon juice
2 cups water
6 cups additional water

Combine first four items. Beat well with a rotary egg beater or electric blender. Add additional water and pour over ice cubes or cracked ice. Serve in tall glasses. Serves 12.

– AUNT MAUD'S RECIPE BOOK from the kitchen of L.M. Montgomery, Elaine Crawford & Kelly Crawford

We placed our precious picnic goodies back into the refrigerator and headed to our destination. It was cold, dull, and damp outside, but the weather just heightened our senses to the warm, bright light that enveloped us as we entered the restaurant. The intoxicating aroma of 11 secret herbs and spices sizzling in the back kitchen tantalized our nostrils, but chicken was not in our budget.

"How much for a large fries and a large gravy?" Randy asked one of the Colonel's lieutenants.

Oh, sweet victory! We had just enough money.

Hurriedly, we climbed back into our gold Ford Fiesta. Time was of the essence. We could not risk our crispy, golden-fried treasure getting cold. As the heat from the cardboard box warmed my lap, the thought of the feast that awaited us warmed both our hearts.

We returned to our humble apartment, collected the remaining picnic provisions, and spread out our picnic blanket on the thinly carpeted cement floor. We placed each picnic item, from the havarti cheese to the green grapes, with care on the blanket. We gave the place of honour in the centre of the blanket to our KFC fries and gravy. We turned on the record player (yes, this was pre-CDs or iPods) and set the repeat dial. Phil Collins' voice filled the room and Randy and I toasted our good fortune.

This is one of my favourite and most cherished memories with my husband. Not only does it make me smile to recall our modest lifestyle, but it inspires me to regain perspective on what's truly important in life. My happiest times did not require an expensive dinner at a white-tablecloth restaurant and a Wine Spectator approved bottle of wine. I didn't need a luxuriously furnished home to feel safe and secure in my husband's arms. I was simply grateful for what I did have.

Today my life is filled with commitments, obligations, responsibilities, and the endless maintenance and acquisition of unnecessary stuff. Often it leaves little time for the things that really matter. Love, joy, and togetherness are the simplest and best of life's gifts. And I believe that the more complex we make our lives – and the more we clutter our homes, our minds, and our days with superfluous stuff – the more unappreciated these gifts are.

That's why, every once in a while, I fill my glass with cheap wine, unwrap the havarti cheese with caraway seeds, wash a bunch of plump, green grapes, turn on the soothing sounds of Phil Collins, and wait for Randy to arrive home with a large order of fries and gravy.

– LOVERS' PICNIC

This exquisite painting is from a manuscript of the Divan (Collected Works) of Hafiz, a fourteenth-century Persian poet. It measures only 7.5 by 4.9 inches and has been attributed to Sultan Muhammad. The inscription above the canopy was written by Hafiz and was translated by Safavid dynasty scholar Martin Bernard Dickson.

It reads:

*A rose without the glow
of a lover bears no joy;
Without wine to drink
the spring brings no joy.*

Photo by Katya Kallsen
© President and Fellows of Harvard College.
Text courtesy of *Harvard Magazine*.

I was simply grateful…

COMPANY BARBECUE

In Good Company

JULY 19, 1987

HOT DOGS
BURGERS

Picnics promise friendship

For some people, work is not a picnic. Perhaps they are performing jobs they find boring and monotonous. Perhaps they dislike their bosses or co-workers. Perhaps their jobs do little to feed their souls, but serve a need to feed their wallets. For others, though, the workplace is a source of pride, inspiration, and camaraderie.

My first big break as a professional writer was to write advertising copy for Lansing Buildall, a lumber and building materials retailer. At first, I couldn't believe my good fortune: someone was actually going to pay me money to put words down on paper. With enthusiasm and zeal, I wrote about lumber and paneling, paint and insulation, lighting and plumbing supplies, and more. I even dressed up as the "Yes, We Wood" girl and visited local newspaper editors to deliver press releases. What a keener I was!

It didn't take long for me to outgrow this junior copywriting role. I tired of writing about the same products over and over again. Composing radio commercials, sales flyers, and newspaper advertisements no longer excited or challenged me. I longed for variety and an opportunity to be more creative.

It was time for me to go. But I did so with a heavy heart. This lumber and building supplies retailer was a family company, both literally and figuratively.

Festivities, food and fun for all! The 1987 Annual Picnic was held July 19th at Seneca College, King Campus. Record crowds attended and joined in on the Water Raft Race, Volleyball Games, Tug-of-War Event, Egg Toss, Bingo, Horseshoes and Suntanning on the Beach. All in all, a fabulous day for the Lansing Family!
– *GOOD WOOD NEWS*,
Lansing Buildall
Company Newsletter

"Atta Girl!"

Here I am in the local newspaper *Abbey's Own* (now *North Oakville Today*), on April 11, 1987.

25 sleeps until our picnic in Pisticci.
Today's Forecast:
Sunny. Warm. Nice.
Temperature of 31°C.
0% chance of precipitation.

Not only did the Kitchen family own and operate the company, they treated each employee as a family member. Going to work each day was warm, comfortable, and familiar. There was a hokey sweetness about the organization. Even the employee performance awards were called "Atta Boy!" and "Atta Girl!" awards. I realize that in today's sophisticated, politically correct world, such titles would be construed as patronizing and overly paternal. But for this company it worked. To complain about it would be like telling a kind old aunt to stop pinching your cheeks.

The thing I missed most after leaving the company was the annual family picnic. A nostalgic journey back in time, this picnic was the highlight of the year. Employees enjoyed barbecued chicken and hotdogs and traditional picnic games, such as horseshoes, volleyball, and tug-of-war. It was a wonderful opportunity for staff to relax and celebrate with their work family and with their actual families. Together.

Why don't more companies host picnics? Certainly cost is a factor, but I think lack of interest and gratitude on the part of the employees also plays a role. A few years ago, I attended another company's annual picnic. What a stark difference it was from the picnics I had come to know and love at Lansing Buildall. The abuse and apathy displayed by the employees created in me a profound sadness and embarrassment for all concerned.

Upon arriving at this picnic, I was pleased to see lots of employees and their families filling the park. All company staff members and their guests were given coupons for various lunch items. To account for possible food preferences, each person received two hamburger coupons, two hotdog coupons, two chicken breast coupons, two barbecued pork coupons, and four beverage coupons. Generous indeed! Imagine my dismay when I saw employees and their families cashing in all of their individual food coupons, filling plastic bags with the excess food, and then promptly leaving the park.

How did these employees even conceive that taking home two hamburgers, two hotdogs, two chicken breasts, two barbecued pork servings, and four cans of soft drinks for each person in their family was somehow acceptable? Where did this sense of entitlement come from?

When you are a guest in someone's home and they serve you a buffet dinner, do you take a plastic bag and fill it with the leftovers? Certainly not.

Perhaps employees don't get that the company for which they work is not a building or a financial statement; it's a group of living, breathing people. It's Terry in shipping, it's Ranjeet in accounting, and it's Anna in customer service; and it is these people who volunteer for the picnic committee, organize the holiday party, or buy the hotdogs for the casual Friday barbecue. Perhaps employees forget that not

Tomato Chickpea Salad

1 can (19 oz.) chickpeas,
    drained and rinsed
1 cup chopped fresh parsley
4 tomatoes,
    cut into chunks
1 cucumber, chopped
6 green onions, sliced
1 cup cubed Swiss cheese*

Dressing
1/3 cup olive oil
3 Tbsp white wine vinegar
1 large clove garlic, crushed
1 tsp dried tarragon leaves
1/2 tsp salt
1/2 tsp dry mustard
1/4 tsp ground black pepper
pinch of cayenne pepper

In large bowl, combine chickpeas, parsley, tomatoes, cucumber, onions and cheese. Dressing: whisk together oil, vinegar, garlic and seasonings. Toss dressing with salad ingredients. Cover and refrigerate several hours. Makes 6 to 8 servings.

*May substitute feta, mozzarella, cheddar or Monterey Jack cheese.

Courtesy of the Ontario Greenhouse Vegetable Growers

"What happens? We go there on buses, see? And when we get there everything is set up – tables, tents, music. And everyone lives it up."

"The hell with the picnics. That's not for us."

– ROADSIDE PICNIC,
Arkady and Boris Strugatsky,
translated by
Antonina W. Bouis

"She didn't like dolls, fairy tales were childish, and one couldn't draw all the time; tea parties didn't amount to much, neither did picnics, unless very well conducted."

– LITTLE WOMEN,
Louisa May Alcott

too long ago, the company they work for was started in someone's spare room, or basement, or kitchen. Perhaps they just don't appreciate that because someone just like them had an idea, a dream, a vision, they now have a job.

Companies don't have to hold picnics, or holiday parties, or casino nights, or treat you to ball games or a day at the amusement park. They don't have to do any of that. They do it to try to make your work environment warm, enjoyable, and inviting.

When employees snub their noses at a company event, they are not only hurting the company that wasted a bunch of money funding it, they are also hurting their fellow workmates who spent long hours organizing it. Most of all, however, these

"Haven't you heard? We're not going to **discuss** the company picnic—this **is** the company picnic."

www.CartoonStock.com

picnic-spoilers, party-poopers, and event-snubbers are hurting themselves.

Cynicism, apathy, ingratitude, and entitlement are not only unattractive and destructive; they rob each of us of joy and a sense of belonging. Our world can be cold and isolating, and we can all use a little more time to relax, play games, talk, laugh, and enjoy great food with our colleagues, our peers, and our families.

…any picnic is a gift

If your company hosts an annual company picnic, consider yourself lucky. If it doesn't, seize the opportunity to organize one. A picnic, any picnic, is a gift. Embrace it. Celebrate it. Enjoy it to the fullest. As the Dalai Lama accurately professes, "Happiness is not something ready made. It comes from your own actions."

Work can be a picnic. We can find happiness, friendship, and a sense of fulfillment at our place of work. But it's up to us to make the effort.

Given the choice of a plastic bag filled with barbecued leftovers or a relaxing, fun-filled afternoon with colleagues and family, I know which I'd choose. But then again, I always did like it when my Aunt Betty pinched my cheeks.

Randy's Barbecue Ribs

Place 4 racks of pork baby back ribs meat side up on a rack in a large roasting pan. Add 2 cups water, cover with foil or lid, and roast for 3 hours at 300°F. Let cool.

1/2 cup ketchup sauce
1 Tbsp brown sugar
1 Tbsp Worcester sauce
1 tsp chili powder
1 Tbsp vinegar
1 tsp paprika
1/2 cup red pepper jelly
1/2 cup honey

Combine all sauce ingredients. With barbecue lid closed, grill ribs at 400-450°F for 2-3 minutes each side. Smother ribs with sauce and grill a few minutes more on each side. For extra saucy ribs, smother and flip ribs again. Serve with plenty of napkins.

Makes 4 to 6 servings.

Feeling Red, White … and Red

"Under this Flag may our youth find new inspiration for loyalty to Canada; for a patriotism based not on any mean or narrow nationalism, but on the deep and equal pride that all Canadians will feel for every part of this good land."

– Prime Minister Lester B. Pearson's Address on the inauguration of the national flag of Canada on February 15, 1965

My son, Mason, at three years old, showing his Canada Day spirit.

Picnics promise patriotism

I admit it. I am jealous of my neighbour to the south. No, not the neighbour that lives one street over – the one that lives below the 49th parallel. My jealousy has nothing to do with the United States of America's power, wealth, or military strength. It has nothing to do with the fact that everything – politics, cable television, big business, college football – appears more exciting in the United States. No, my jealousy has more to do with the American flag. It's not that I prefer stars and stripes to a red maple leaf. It's not that I begrudge the United States of America the colour blue versus our limited colour scheme of red and white. I am jealous because, in my humble opinion, the people of the United States wave their flag more vigorously than we do in Canada.

Before my fellow Canadians get their beaver tails bent out of shape or their toques in a twist, or start looking for their Vancouver 2010 red mittens, answer this question: How did you last celebrate your country's birthday?

I am not talking about enjoying an extra day at the family cottage, securing an early tee time, or lying by the pool. And I am most certainly not talking about an extra day to catch up on the laundry, cut the lawn, or return emails! Did you actually do something to commemorate and celebrate the birth of your country?

> "As Canadians I think we have an ability to celebrate being so ordinary that we're 'extra ordinary'."
>
> – Jann Arden, singer, songwriter, and author, as quoted in *Canadian Health & Lifestyle*.
> www.healthandlifestyle.ca

"9:30: Pledge allegiance. 10: Wave flag. 10:30: Sing 'Yankee Doodle.' 11: Show true colors. 11:30: Sing 'God Bless America.' 12: Picnic lunch. 1:30: Wave flag again...."

© Henry Martin
The New Yorker Collection
www.cartoonbank.com

"When Canadians compete we don't compete to conquer. We compete to achieve and celebrate something…"

– Jon Montgomery, Olympic gold medalist, as quoted in *Canadian Health & Lifestyle*.
www.healthandlifestyle.ca

It's my personal observation that new Canadians do a better job celebrating Canada Day than Canadians by birth. Maybe it's because they know firsthand that all countries are not created equal. Maybe new Canadians know how truly blessed we are to live in a country that is glorious and free. When I was growing up, my father would give thanks at Thanksgiving dinner for our many blessings. As my sisters and I looked longingly at the turkey and roast potatoes getting cold, he would give thanks for the food we were about to eat, our family, our good health, our home – and he always, always, gave thanks for the country in which we live. It wasn't until I became an adult that I realized how lucky I am to live in Canada.

My husband and I have tried to instill a love of country in our two children. Over the years, we hosted Canada Day barbecues with road hockey matches. We attended Canada Day community events and fireworks displays. But all things considered, I believe I experienced the greatest feeling of patriotism when the four of us celebrated our first Canada Day together.

It was July 1, 1994, a gorgeous summer day. The sky was a brilliant blue and the sun was shining brightly. It was Canada Day and we had no plans. I remember thinking that this lack of plans was completely unacceptable. I didn't care how tired I was from caring for my young family. My son, Mason, was just three years old and my daughter, Kinsey,

Canada Day Picnic Sandwich

by The Canadian Living Magazine Test Kitchen

1 loaf bread (round, crusty)
1/2 cup (125 mL) mayonnaise (approx.)
3 cups (750 mL) cubed cooked chicken
1 cup (250 mL) green grapes, halved
1/2 cup (125 mL) chopped celery
1/2 cup (125 mL) toasted sliced almonds
1/4 cup (50 mL) sliced green onions
salt and pepper
romaine lettuce
1 sweet red pepper, slivered

Cut top off loaf. Hollow out bread, leaving 1/2-inch (1 cm) shell. Mix together 1/3 cup (75 mL) of the mayonnaise, chicken, grapes, celery, almonds, onions, and salt and pepper to taste. Brush the shell generously with remaining mayonnaise and line with lettuce. Spoon about two-thirds of the chicken mixture into romaine-lined shell. Layer slivered red pepper over salad; spoon remaining chicken mixture on top. Replace bread top. Wrap sandwich tightly in plastic and refrigerate until picnic time. (Cut in wedges.) Makes 6 servings.

© *Canadian Living*

"Canada, our Canada is truly worthy of our pride and our patriotism … We will ask the world to forgive us this uncharacteristic outburst of patriotism, of our pride, to be part of a country that is strong, confident and tall among the nations."

– Statement by the Prime Minister of Canada, Stephen Harper, February 11, 2010

was less than a year old. I didn't care that my husband, Randy, had had a busy week at work. We could not let Canada Day pass without celebrating. We needed a picnic!

I grabbed a blanket and filled a cooler with whatever I could find in the refrigerator. Randy grabbed a duffle bag and filled it with sports equipment. Mason got the little Canadian flag he had made at preschool and sat on the stairs, waiting patiently for the celebration to begin.

Fourth of July picnics are an iconic symbol of U.S. patriotism. The fried chicken, the potato salad, the watermelon, and the lemonade are as American as apple pie. Independence Day picnics are featured in books, movies, and television programs time and again. As a Canadian, I sometimes feel I am missing out on something. But on that day, as my family and I played on the swings, skipped stones on Lake Ontario, munched on our peanut butter sandwiches, and shooed away the Canada geese while dodging their droppings, I felt proud. I felt patriotic. I felt love for my country! Most of all, I felt red, white, and Canadian all over.

My husband, Randy, and our two children, Mason and Kinsey, enjoy a Canada Day picnic in Oakville, Ontario.

I felt love for my country…

"Make the pursuit of happiness real and personal: hang and wave the flag; find a local parade and then share loaves and fishes with family and friends at an old-fashioned potluck picnic. Watch the fireworks in the evening or set off your own authentic sparks. Declare your personal independence…"

– *SIMPLE ABUNDANCE,*
A Daybook of Comfort and Joy,
Sarah Ban Breathnach

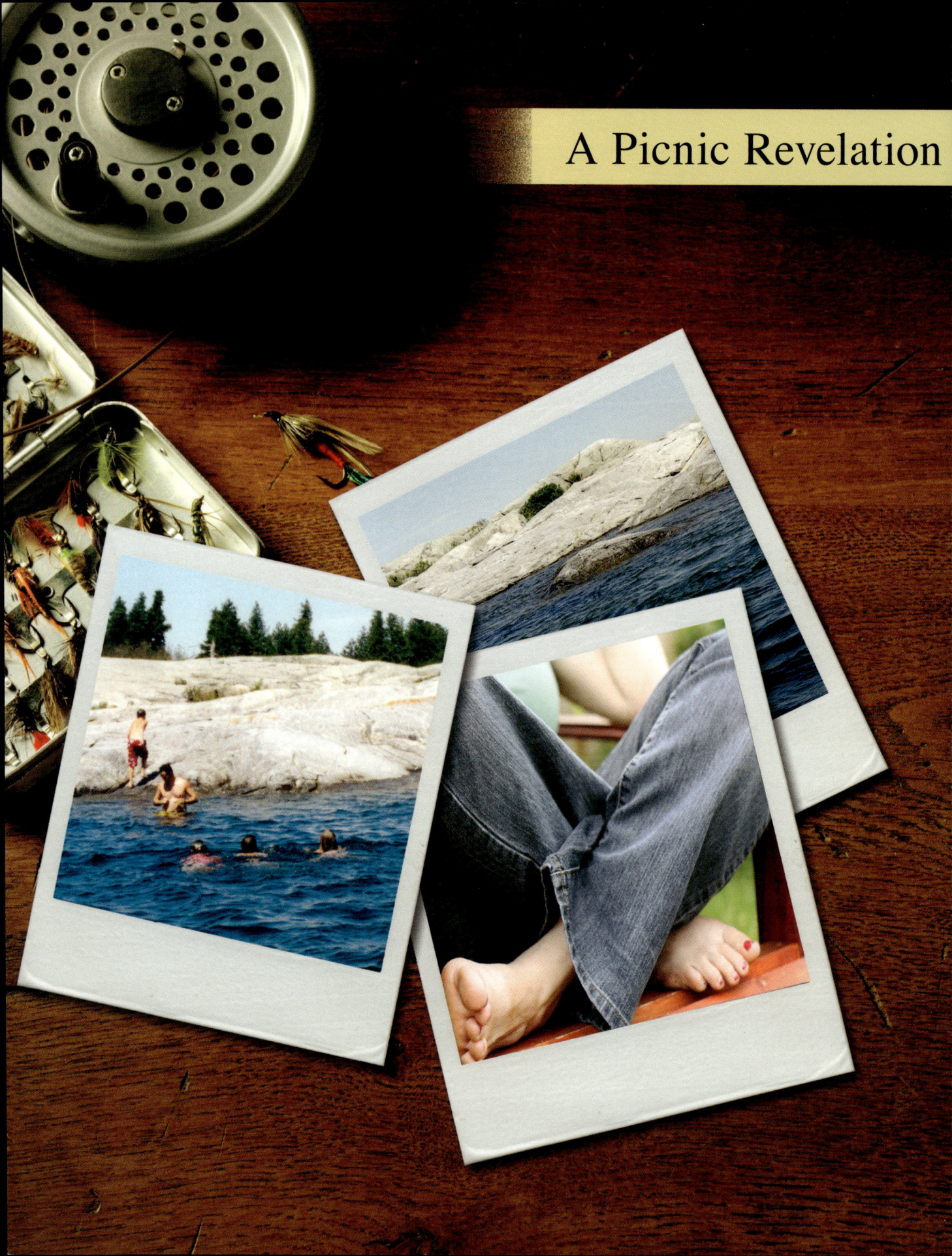

A Picnic Revelation

Picnics promise adventure

I pride myself on being a supportive and loving wife. My husband, Randy, has enjoyed great success in his business career and I have tried hard to be an asset to him when we attend business functions together. Now before anyone sets her bra ablaze, Randy has played the role of Mr. Tina Powell on many occasions. We support each other – a kind of career *quid pro quo*. So when Randy told me that we were invited for a day trip to his boss's cottage, I was delighted to accept the invitation. After eating countless rubber chicken dinners over the years, I welcomed the thought of a family outing in cottage country: boating, swimming, and barbecuing. It was my kind of corporate commitment.

When we arrived at the cottage on a spectacular July day, we discovered that our hosts had planned a surprise for us. We were going to have a picnic lunch on an island! They had packed a large cooler of sandwich fixings, beverages, and fresh fruit, and they knew of a perfect island destination. Everyone was thrilled. Everyone except me.

Not to be ungrateful, but we had just driven for three hours to get to the marina, where we met up with our hosts, who then drove us in their motorboat

If you go down
in the woods today
You're sure of a
big surprise.
If you go down
in the woods today
You'd better go
in disguise;
For ev'ry Bear that
ever there was
Will gather there
for certain because
Today's the day
the Teddy Bears
have their picnic.
Picnic time for
Teddy Bears.
The little Teddy Bears
are having a lovely time
today. Watch them,
catch them unawares
And see them picnic
on their holiday.

– *THE TEDDY BEARS' PICNIC*, lyrics by Jimmy Kennedy

"You must live in the present, launch yourself on every wave, find your eternity in each moment."

– Henry David Thoreau, from his journal, April 24, 1859

20 sleeps until our picnic in Pisticci.

Today's Forecast:

More sun than clouds.

Warm. Temperature of 30°C.

30% chance of precipitation.

to the cottage. Now they were telling me that I had to change out of my cute little cottage outfit – which they saw for all of five minutes – put on a bathing suit, take off my makeup, and get into another boat! This was not what I'd had in mind. I was supposed to be lounging on a big, cedar deck, sipping chilled white wine, nibbling on gourmet delicacies. But I smiled my corporate wife smile and said, "An island picnic? How wonderful!"

To my surprise, on the way to the island, I actually started to enjoy myself. The sun was shining, the kids were having a fabulous time bouncing in the bow with each wave, and the fresh air and open water were exhilarating. Maybe this island picnic wasn't such a bad idea after all.

As we neared our island oasis, our host suddenly cut the engine of the boat. "This is as close as I can get," he announced. "The water is just too choppy."

We were a long way from shore. His wife frowned and suggested, "Maybe we should go to Henry's instead?"

Henry's is a popular fish restaurant in the area. I said a silent prayer, "Please, God, let us go to Henry's." I could almost taste the lightly battered fish and the crisp golden fries. Was that malt vinegar I smelled?

"No, I'll anchor here and we'll swim ashore," he replied.

Did he say swim? I am not much of a swimmer. I've never had formal swimming lessons and although I spent my childhood summer holidays at Wasaga Beach, the numerous sandbars kept my head above water and my feet firmly on the ground.

"What about lunch?" I thought. "Nobody likes a soggy sandwich." I watched in dismay as the picnic cooler was lowered into the water. Imagine that. Someone actually invented a floating cooler. Thanks for nothing, whoever you are.

Eyeing the choppy waves, his wife pushed, "Maybe Randy and Tina don't want the kids to swim to shore." Ah, finally a voice of reason. Now all that needed to happen was Randy to agree and it would be fish and chips all around. I tried to give him that penetrating spousal stare that makes words unnecessary.

"No worries," I heard my husband say, "Mason and Kinsey are great swimmers!"

"It's settled," our host commanded. "Everybody in!"

I grabbed Randy's arm and locked eyes with his. "You need to swim with the children," I said through clenched teeth and a frozen smile. "I will not be able to help them if they have trouble."

Randy shrugged his shoulders. "Sure, no problem." Clearly, he did not get the underlying message that only a drowning mother would be unwilling or unable to save her own children.

"One compensation of old age is that it excuses you from picnics."
– William Feather, American publisher and author

Scene from the movie *Picnic*, 1955. mptvimages.com

"Mrs. Potts: I think we plan picnics just to give ourselves an excuse … to let something thrilling and romantic happen to us –"
From the play, *PICNIC*, by William Inge

Tina's Breaded Chicken Wings

2 lb chicken wing drumettes and/or wingettes
1 cup all-purpose flour
1 cup milk
2 cups bread crumbs
2 tsp garlic salt
2 tsp paprika
2 tsp black pepper
2 tsp curry powder
2 Tbsp grated Parmesan cheese
1 lemon

Preheat oven to 350°F. Line large cookie sheet with foil. In a small bowl, place flour. In a separate bowl, pour milk. In a third bowl, combine bread crumbs, spices, and cheese. Rinse wings with cold water. Roll each piece in flour, dip in milk, and then coat with bread crumb mixture. Place coated chicken pieces on cookie sheet, leaving room between each piece for equal browning. Bake for 45 minutes until brown and crispy. Cool to touch, place in airtight container, and then chill in refrigerator for several hours or overnight. Drizzle with fresh-squeezed lemon juice and serve.

Splash! Splash! Splash! Bodies dove into the dark, wavy water. I looked toward the rocky shore. As that shore receded farther into the horizon (in my mind), I prayed to wake from this nightmare. I slowly raised my bathing suit cover-up over my head. It was such a pretty bathing suit: a floral skirt bottom and a snug, bikini top. This was not the type of suit swimmers wore to cross the English Channel. Furthermore, my curvy physique would do little to generate aerodynamic speed through the swirling water.

The last one out of the boat was me. I took a deep breath and plunged into the chilling water. Once I surfaced, I flailed my arms like a double-jointed windmill. I kicked my legs like a battery-operated cancan dancer. I gasped for air like a clogged vacuum cleaner. Suddenly, my cold, wet hand

From the boat, I surveyed the magnitude of the swim before me and silently cursed the inventor of the floating cooler.

made contact with a warm, dry rock. I had made it. I was going to live! My children would not be motherless after all. My heart burst with pride and joy. I felt like an Olympic swimmer winning gold.

Rather than exhausted, I felt energized. I was mighty. I was invincible. I was the greatest swimmer in the world! I was ready to explode out of the water and onto the shore in a style befitting such a tremendous physical feat! But for some reason – thank you, thank you, God – I hesitated. Something didn't feel quite right. I felt below the water. Somehow my bathing suit top had become my bathing suit necklace. I had narrowly escaped flashing my husband's boss, his wife, and their children.

I gasped for air...

I sunk back into the water, put the girls back into place, and emerged with the grace and elegance befitting the Olympic champion I now was.

As I warmed my body against the rocky shore, nibbled on sandwiches, and listened to the lively conversation, I realized something: I was powerful. My body was strong. My mind was tough. If I really tried, I could do and overcome anything. Then a sinking feeling came over me. How would I ever get back to the boat?

The Rat brought the boat alongside the bank, made her fast, helped the still awkward Mole safely ashore, and swung out the luncheon-basket. The Mole begged as a favour to be allowed to unpack it all by himself; and the Rat was very pleased to indulge him, and to sprawl at full length on the grass and rest, while his excited friend shook out the tablecloth and spread it, took out all the mysterious packets one by one and arranged their contents in due order, still gasping, 'O my! O my!' at each fresh revelation.

– *THE WIND IN THE WILLOWS*, Kenneth Grahame
Illustrated by Ernest H. Shepard

Home Is Where the Picnic Is

Picnics promise Family

"I will not live and die within a 100-mile radius of where I was born." This was the pledge that my husband and I made to each other when we first married. It's a great pledge, but in truth, we were still living 20 minutes down the highway from Toronto, where both of us were born.

Over the years, Randy's work has provided ample opportunity for us to relocate, but we always had what we believed to be reasonable objections to moving. As cautious Canadians, we were a little bit afraid of some of the U.S. cities at our access. Tales of local crack houses, parking lot robberies, and gang warfare kept our overly polite, parka-clad butts safe and sound above the 49th parallel. Invitations to move to South America, Mexico, and Tokyo were met with little enthusiasm. Will the schools be good? How will we manage without knowing the language? What do you mean the position includes a staff of personal bodyguards?

In our mid-forties (heavy on the mid part), it appeared we were destined to live and die within that 100-mile radius. But then the unexpected happened. We got an offer that, as Marlon Brando once mumbled, we just couldn't refuse. Try as we might, we could not come up with a reasonable objection to moving to Vancouver, Canada. Okay,

"I'd made up a little basket, just a little, fair-sized basket, an ordinary biggish sort of basket, full of –"
– *THE HOUSE AT POOH CORNER*,
A.A. Milne
Illustrated by E.H. Shepard

so maybe it wasn't the most exotic of locales, but it was clear across the country and over 2,000 miles away from home!

How far can a mother's

On September 8th, we made our decision to accept the job offered to Randy. On September 12th, I was on an airplane headed to my new home. Having never relocated before, I had no idea what to expect. I was the proverbial deer in the headlights. Selling our home, finding a new home, securing temporary housing, obtaining new driver's licences, changing over health plans, and enrolling Kinsey in high school were just some of the tasks I had ahead of me.

Overlooking the city of Vancouver, we picnicked in our new home.

On top of it all, Mason decided that he wanted to finish his high school education in the Toronto area. Not only were we leaving all our friends and family, I was also leaving my baby boy. My family was splitting up. How far can a mother's arms reach?

Unless you have relocated to another city, you don't realize all the little things you take for granted: where you bank, who cuts your hair, having a dentist and a doctor, where you buy your groceries, knowing which bakery has the freshest bread, where to find the best sushi. You also

16 sleeps until our picnic in Pisticci.
Today's Forecast:
Sunny. Warm.
Temperature of 30°C.
0% chance of precipitation.

take for granted knowing the street names the traffic reporters list on the radio. For months, I would listen to traffic reports and have no idea whether I

arms reach...

was driving right towards a major traffic jam. More importantly, you take for granted being able to visit your mom or dad whenever you please, or grab an impromptu dinner with friends, or kiss your son goodnight.

It took a few months, but I got my bearings fairly quickly and found that there were many things to love about my new city. The mountains are majestic, the ocean is breathtaking, the vegetation is green and lush, and the weather is mild, though a little wetter than I am used to. The city is vibrant, with great shopping and world-class restaurants. I even found a house for my family and we were scheduled to take possession on January 2nd. Not bad for less than four months' work!

After spending a lovely Christmas week in Ontario with family and friends, we collected our son and returned to Vancouver on January 2nd. We weren't actually scheduled to move in until mid-February, but we were anxious to show Mason our new home. The more I thought about it, however, the less excited I got. It seemed awfully

My Sister-in-Law Donna's Delectable Brownies

3/4 cup flour
1/3 cup cocoa
1/4 tsp salt
1 cup sugar
1/2 cup butter
2 eggs
3 Tbsp water
1 tsp vanilla

Preheat oven to 325°F. Grease 8" square pan. In a large bowl, blend together first four ingredients. Add remaining ingredients and beat with electric mixer. Stir in 1/2 cup nuts if desired. Pour in greased pan and bake for 25 to 30 minutes. Once they are cool, you can spread icing on top or sprinkle with icing sugar, but they are wonderful just plain.

My family toasts a successful move to Vancouver.

anti-climactic to walk into an empty house after all we had been through. We didn't have a chair to sit in or a pot to … boil water in.

As I sat on the plane, looking at my precious family – my husband, my daughter, and my son – by my side, I realized furniture is overrated. From the Vancouver airport, we drove directly to our rented condo, grabbed a blanket from the sofa, stopped at Whole Foods, and then hurried to our new home.

Sitting on the hardwood floor, looking out the window at the view, we munched on cold breaded chicken, salads, sushi, and fruit.

My heart burst with joy…

My husband and I and our picnic smooch.

We chatted. We laughed. We made plans. My heart burst with joy. I knew it didn't matter whether I was in Toronto or Vancouver, in the United States, South America, Mexico, or Asia. As long as I had my husband, my children, and a picnic blanket, I was home.

"Some for me and some for you," says bunny one to bunny two.
Bunny three and bunny four say, "Pass us seconds. We'd like more."
Bunny five and bunny six shout, "Hooray for night picnics!"

– *THE BUNNIES' PICNIC*, Lezlie Evans
Illustrated by Kay Chorao

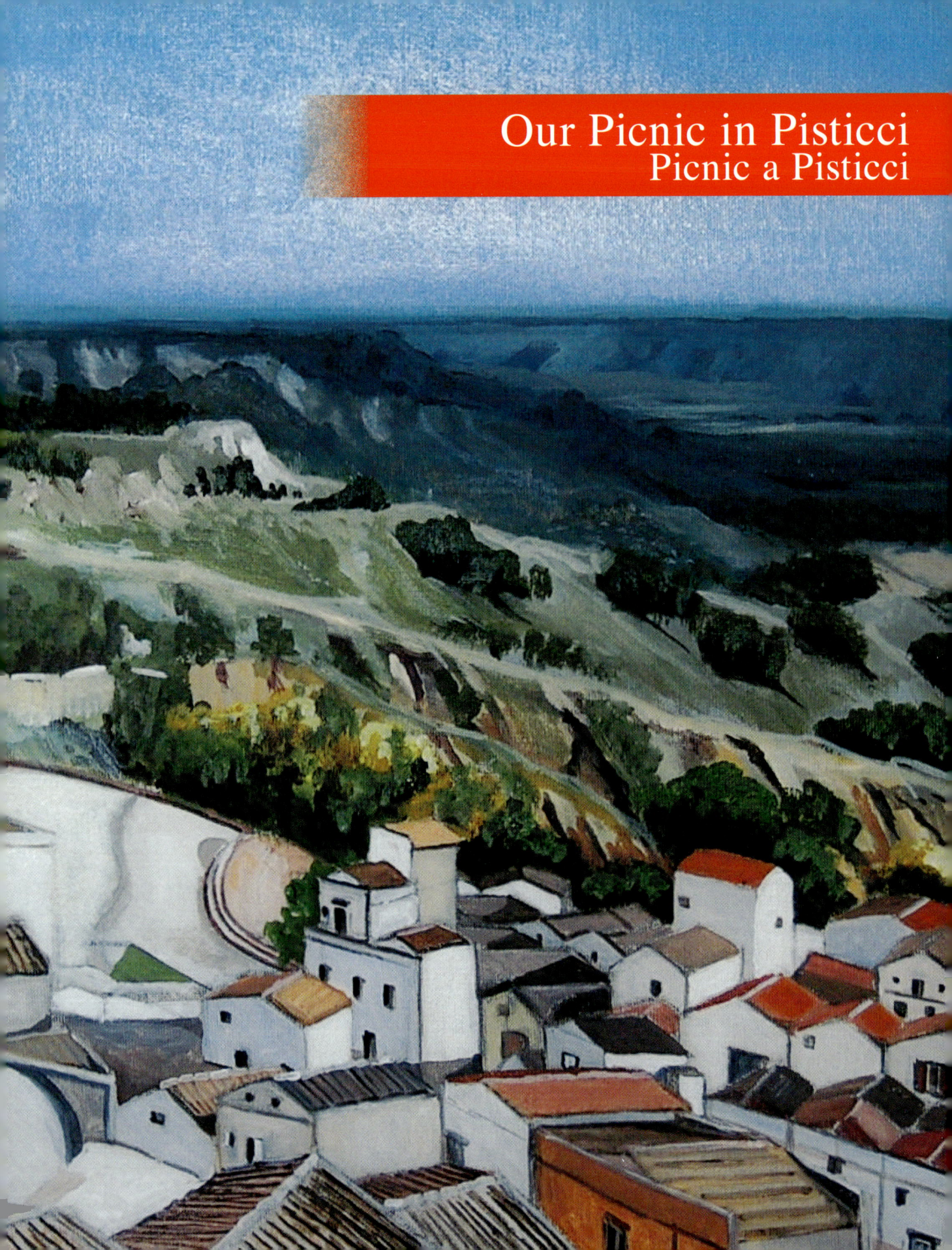

Our Picnic in Pisticci
Picnic a Pisticci

Picnics promise perfection

It is July 19th. After seven months of planning and anticipation, our picnic in Pisticci is just two days away. My family and I arrived in Italy nine days ago. We began our journey in Venice, made our way to Florence, and we are now travelling by train through Naples to the town of Pisticci. Rome will follow, but today all we can think about is Pisticci.

On the train, I am literally sandwiched between two generations of D'Alessandros. On one side are my children, Mason and Kinsey, and on the other is my father, James D'Alessandro.

È il 19 luglio. Il fatidico giorno è ormai alle porte: dopo sette mesi di preparativi e aspettative, mancano solo due giorni al picnic a Pisticci. Insieme a tutta la mia famiglia, siamo arrivati in Italia nove giorni fa. Siamo partiti da Venezia, poi ci siamo fermati a Firenze e ora siamo in treno, diretti a Napoli e da lì a Pisticci.

Poi andremo anche a Roma, ma oggi c'è solo Pisticci nei nostri pensieri. Mentre mi guardo intorno, mi rendo conto di essere letteralmente presa in mezzo tra due generazioni di D'Alessandro: da una parte i miei figli, Mason e Kinsey, dall'altra mio padre, James D'Alessandro.

Opposite Page:
"View from Pisticci"
by Anne Parker

"Charmed by the tidy beauty of the place, by the houses all the same…"

– *Alla ricerca di Rocco e i suoi fratelli: la Basilicata di Luchino Visconti,* Teresa Megale, from Pisticci tourism map / brochure

My father, James D'Alessandro, arrives in his father's hometown of Pisticci for the first time.

My mangia-cake husband, Randy, has graciously agreed to share our summer vacation with my father and his fiancée, Lily Frutti. As the scenery races by and we head further south, our excitement builds. Today is the first time that anyone from my immediate family has visited my grandparents' hometown.

My father paces up and down the aisle, looks out the window, checks his watch, and then paces some more. To my family, Pisticci was some faraway land, rich in family history and stories but completely out of reach. I couldn't wait to see my father's face when he stepped off the train in Pisticci.

Mio marito Randy, canadese "doc", ha gentilmente accettato di passare le vacanze estive con mio padre e la sua compagna, Lily Frutti. Mentre il panorama scorre veloce fuori dal finestrino e scendiamo verso sud, l'eccitazione è sempre più palpabile. Siamo tutti gasatissimi: questa è la prima volta che la mia famiglia, intendendo i parenti più stretti, viene nella città natale dei miei nonni.

Mio padre cammina nervosamente su e giù per il corridoio, un'occhiata fuori dal finestrino, poi uno sguardo all'orologio, e poi ancora su e giù, avanti e indietro, agitato. Per i miei, Pisticci è sempre stato un paese lontano, ricco di storia di famiglia e di racconti, ma quasi irraggiungibile. Non vedevo l'ora di vedere la faccia di mio padre quando, sceso dal treno, avrebbe messo finalmente il piede a terra a Pisticci.

"White clay without trees or grass … like a lunar landscape … precipices … on which the houses stayed as if they were hovering in the air."
– *Cristo si è fermato ad Eboli*, Carlo Levi, from Pisticci tourism map / brochure

When I wake picnic day morning, I open the door of my tiny room at Club Med Metaponto and brilliant sunshine explodes around me. It's blinding. I shut my eyes and then the door. Despite the spectacular weather, I do not have high hopes for our picnic in Pisticci. After spending the previous day getting our bearings in this small southern Italian town, I realized that finding an ideal picnic spot would be nearly impossible.

Located in the region of Basilicata, in the province of Matera, Pisticci is a small town of just under 18,000 people. Its name comes from the Latin word *pesticius*, meaning pasture land, but the town itself consists of row upon row of white houses and stone laneways with very little grass or protection from the Mediterranean sun. No grass. No shade.

No grass. No shade...

Quando mi sveglio, la mattina del giorno in cui abbiamo programmato il picnic, apro la porta e una luce abbagliante inonda la piccola camera del Club Med Metaponto. Accecata dai raggi del sole, chiudo gli occhi e accompagno la porta. Nonostante la giornata si annunci fantastica, non nutro molte speranze per il picnic a Pisticci. Dopo aver trascorso la giornata di ieri a prendere confidenza con il posto e ad orientarci in questa cittadina dell'Italia del sud, mi sono resa conto che trovare il luogo ideale per il picnic sarebbe stato praticamente impossibile.

Pisticci è una cittadina di poco meno di 18.000 abitanti in provincia di Matera, in Basilicata. Il nome deriva dal latino pesticius, terreno a pascolo, ma il paese è un susseguirsi di case bianche, una fila dopo l'altra, e strade lastricate in pietra dove non vi è quasi nemmeno un filo d'erba né il minimo riparo dal caldo sole mediterraneo. Non c'è l'erba. Non c'è l'ombra.

Today's Forecast:
Sunny. Hot!
Temperature of 40ºC.
0% chance of precipitation.

Another concern is time. This may very well be my father's one and only visit to his parents' place of birth. Understandably, there are many things he wants to do and see. He wants to visit the municipal office to research his ancestors. He wants to see the street on which his father was born and the church in which he worshipped. He wants to visit cousins he's never met, walk the streets, eat gelato, and drink wine. The list goes on.

I sit on the edge of my bed. My visions of the perfect picnic in Pisticci begin to dissipate. I start to

...walk the streets, eat gelato, and drink wine

E poi il fattore tempo. Questa è molto probabilmente la prima e unica volta che mio padre visita la città natale dei suoi genitori. È comprensibile che voglia fare e vedere tante cose: andare in comune per cercare informazioni sui suoi antenati; camminare lungo la strada in cui nacque mio nonno e visitare la chiesa in cui andava a pregare; andare a trovare i cugini che non ha mai conosciuto; e poi passeggiare, mangiare il gelato e bere il vino. E chissà quant'altro ancora.

Sto seduta sul ciglio del letto. L'idea che mi ero fatta del perfetto picnic a Pisticci comincia piano piano a sgretolarsi.

consider alternative ideas. "Perhaps we could just have a nice lunch at a roadside café," I think. "Perhaps my book could be titled Pizza in Pisticci." I frown. Somehow it doesn't have the same panache. I decide to persevere with the picnic.

I fold and pack the spare blanket in my room. At least I have a picnic blanket. That's a start. Next I need cups, plates, utensils, and napkins. Surely I can borrow these items from the resort. I visit the front reception desk and explain my picnic predicament. The woman behind the counter shakes her head and says, "No, I am sorry. Maybe you can make a sandwich at the breakfast buffet and take it with you." No, no, no, no, that won't do at all.

On the way to the waiting car, I steal six disposable plastic cups from the poolside bar (now I'm resorting to a life of crime). Disappointed in myself and

Penso a delle alternative. "Magari potremmo fare un pranzo veloce in un baretto lungo la strada", mi dico. "E in tal caso potrei intitolare il mio libro Pizza a Pisticci." No, non funziona, dico tra me e me con espressione accigliata.

Non sembra essere altrettanto evocante. Allora, se picnic deve essere, picnic sia. Piego e metto via la coperta in più che fa parte della dotazione della camera. La coperta ce l'abbiamo. È già un buon inizio. Poi mi servono bicchieri, piatti, posate, tovaglioli. Ma sì, li posso chiedere all'albergo. Vado al banco della reception e spiego le mie esigenze. L'impiegata scuote la testa e gentilmente risponde: "No, mi dispiace non posso aiutarla. Forse può preparare dei panini al buffet della colazione e portarli con sé." No, no, no e poi no, così non si può.

Mentre mi dirigo verso la macchina dove il resto della famiglia mi sta aspettando, passando davanti al bar della piscina, prendo sei bicchieri di carta dal bancone (mi sono ridotta a fare la ladra!). Delusa da me stessa e

The perfect way to begin any day!

Doppio
A double shot of espresso. (Doppio means double in Italian.)

Espresso macchiato
A single serving of espresso topped with a dollop of frothed milk.

Espresso con panna
A single espresso topped with a dollop of whipped cream.

in the day, I climb into the car with my blanket and six plastic cups. Some picnic this is going to be! No grass. No shade. No time. No provisions.

Fifteen minutes later, we arrive in Pisticci and my spirits begin to lift. While Dad and Lily head to the municipal office, Randy, the kids, and I find a small café. As Randy and I savour strong espresso and light pastry (the perfect way to begin any day), we watch the town come alive. Residents happily greet each other in the morning sun. I can't help but compare this scene to the stream of robotic commuters and office workers I normally see back home.

Suddenly, my jubilant father appears with a fistful of official-looking documents. We all marvel at the efficiency of Pisticci's small municipal office.

pronta per vivere la grande giornata, salgo in macchina con la coperta e sei bicchieri di carta. Ma che bel picnic ci attende! Non c'è l'erba. Non c'è l'ombra. Non c'è tempo. E non c'è nulla da mangiare.

Quando dopo un breve tragitto di un quarto d'ora arriviamo a Pisticci, lo spirito a poco a poco si rianima. Mentre papà e Lily s'incamminano verso il comune, i bambini e io scoviamo un piccolo caffè. Randy e io ordiniamo un espresso forte e dei dolcetti leggeri (l'ideale per cominciare la giornata) e ci divertiamo ad osservare la vita animata intorno a noi. Tutti si salutano amabilmente sotto i raggi del sole mattutino. Non posso non paragonare la scena all'andirivieni di pendolari e impiegati che camminano come automi ogni mattina lungo i marciapiedi delle strade della mia città.

Ecco che sbuca fuori mio padre, che, esultante, sventola dei fogli che hanno tutta l'aria di essere documenti ufficiali. Tutti restiamo stupiti dell'efficienza del piccolo ufficio comunale di Pisticci.

"What could be simpler: shop, travel to your chosen destination, spread out the rug, pour a drink, and let everyone unwrap your treasures and enjoy your easy, inspirational, open air picnic."

– *FOOD FOR FRIENDS:*
Simply Delicious Menus for Easy Entertaining,
Fran Warde

We leave the comfort of the air-conditioned café and make our way along the town's main street. The air is warm and still. I glance upwards at a sign hanging above the drugstore. I gasp. It's not yet noon and it's already 35° Celsius! No grass. No shade. No time. No provisions. No point.

Disheartened, I wonder whether our picnic in Pisticci is doomed. I seriously consider giving up, but can't bring myself to do it. Today is July 21st. Today is the anniversary of my grandfather's birth. Today is the day we must have a picnic in Pisticci!

Lasciamo la piacevole atmosfera del bar (e il fresco dell'aria condizionata) per incamminarci lungo il "corso". L'aria è calda e soffocante. Mi vanno gli occhi su un tabellone in evidenza sulla porta di un negozio di alimentari. Boccheggio. Non è ancora mezzogiorno e già ci sono 35 gradi! Non c'è l'erba. Non c'è l'ombra. Non c'è tempo. Non c'è nulla da mangiare.

E non c'è nemmeno un posto dove fare il picnic. Demoralizzata, mi chiedo se il nostro picnic a Pisticci sia nato sotto una cattiva stella. Penso seriamente di lasciar perdere, ma è più forte di me, non posso. Oggi è il 21 luglio. Oggi è l'anniversario della nascita di mio nonno. Oggi è il giorno in cui dobbiamo fare il picnic a Pisticci!

We enlist the help of Agostino, our Pisticci taxi-driver-turned-tour-guide. We share our picnic plans with Agostino and he shakes his head. "No pic-a-nic," he says. "Ristorante!" We all laugh, and Lily, who has been our translator and lifeline throughout the entire trip, explains in Italian that I am writing a book about having a picnic in Pisticci and that I must have a picnic in Pisticci.

That is all Agostino needs to hear. "Sì, sì. Pic-a-nic!" he smiles.

All will be well, but before we can have our picnic, we have to make one more very important stop. We must visit the street where my grandfather, John D'Alessandro, was born. We must visit #19 Via Galilei. But suddenly Agostino's cell phone rings.

Sì, sì. Pic-a-nic...

Chiediamo aiuto ad Agostino, il nostro autista di Pisticci tramutato in guida turistica. Gli raccontiamo i nostri programmi per la giornata, ma Agostino scuote la testa "Ma quale pic-a-nic" dice. "Ristorante!" Scoppiamo tutti a ridere e Lily, che ha fatto da interprete ed è stata l'ancora di salvezza per tutto il viaggio, spiega in italiano che sto scrivendo un libro in cui racconto di un picnic a Pisticci e quindi dobbiamo fare un picnic a Pisticci.

Agostino non ha bisogno di sentire altro. "Sì, sì. Pic-a-nic!" sorride.

Andrà tutto bene, ma prima del picnic, dobbiamo fare un'altra sosta molto importante. Dobbiamo vedere la strada in cui nacque mio nonno, Giovanni D'Alessandro, e fermarci in Via Galilei 19. Ma ad un tratto squilla il cellulare di Agostino.

Agostino serenades my family while he drives.

Santa Lucia
(A Song of Naples)

Sul mare luccica
l'astro d'argento.
Placida è l'onda.
Prospero è il vento.
Sul mare luccica,
l'astro d'argento.
Placida è l'onda.
Prospero è il vento.
Venite all'agile,
barchetta mia,
Santa Lucia,
Santa Lucia.
Venite all'agile,
barchetta mia,
Santa Lucia,
Santa Lucia.

– Traditional Neapolitan folk song transcribed by Teodoro Cottrau

Agostino answers the call. Apparently, my father's cousin Santino is looking for us in the town square. Although Santino was aware that my family was coming to Italy, he did not know the exact timing of our trip. Through a chain of communication that would have impressed the inventors of the Internet, Santino found out that we were with Agostino.

Santino meets up with us just as we are leaving my grandfather's street. He is eager to take us to meet other relatives in town, but is told about my desire to create the perfect picnic in Pisticci. His eyes open wide and there is little doubt in my mind that he thinks I am certifiably insane. But I don't care. I am in Pisticci and I am going to have my picnic! Santino joins us on our quest.

My children, Mason and Kinsey, take a break from the sun with their grandfather and our extraordinary taxi driver, Agostino Laviola.

A quanto pare, il cugino di mio padre, Santino, ci cerca in piazza. Santino era a conoscenza del nostro viaggio in Italia, ma non sapeva esattamente quando saremmo venuti. Attraverso un passaparola che avrebbe fatto impallidire gli inventori di internet, Santino aveva saputo che eravamo con Agostino.

Santino ci raggiunge proprio mentre stiamo lasciando via Galilei. Ci tiene tanto a farci conoscere gli altri parenti, ma lo informiamo del mio desiderio di vivere l'esperienza del picnic a Pisticci. A queste parole, sgrana gli occhi e non ho dubbi che abbia pensato che dovevo essere pazza. Ma non m'interessa. Sono a Pisticci e farò il picnic, costi quel che costi! Santino accetta l'invito di unirsi a noi.

The first thing we need is a location. Agostino and Santino argue back and forth in Italian for a few moments. Eventually, they agree upon the park at Villa Comunale. Next we need food. Agostino leads us through the stifling heat to a small market. The shopkeeper welcomes us with glasses of chilled meloncello (a much sweeter sister to limoncello). As the cool liqueur soothes my parched throat, I catch sight of the wonderful array of Italian delicacies that fill the market. A wave of relief washes over me.

The merchant is told of our mission and he immediately sets to work. "What you want?" he asks.

La prima cosa che ci serve è un posto. Agostino e Santino, dopo aver discusso in italiano per qualche minuto, di comune accordo suggeriscono il parco della Villa Comunale. Poi dobbiamo procurarci da mangiare. Agostino ci accompagna ad un piccolo supermercato. Nel frattempo, si fa sempre più caldo. Il titolare del negozio ci offre gentilmente un bicchierino di meloncello (il fratello molto più dolce del limoncello) ghiacciato. Mentre il liquore mi rinfresca la gola, mi vanno gli occhi sulla meravigliosa serie di squisitezze italiane in esposizione intorno a me.

Mi sento molto rincuorata. Spieghiamo al negoziante la nostra intenzione e subito si mette a nostra disposizione. "Che volete?" chiede.

Merchant Rocco Nicodemo saves the day with fresh meats, cheese, bread, olives, watermelon, and chilled white wine.

My Dad's Peppers and Eggs Sandwich

1/4 cup of canola and olive oil blend, enough to cover bottom of frying pan

1 clove of garlic, chopped finely

4 green or red peppers, washed, seeded, and sliced in strips

6 large eggs, beaten with 1 Tbsp of milk

salt and pepper to taste

In a non-stick frying pan add oil and garlic. Sauté on low to medium heat until lightly browned. Add peppers and cook, stirring often, until peppers start to soften. Adjust heat to medium-high and add egg mixture. Coat peppers completely with eggs and stir gently. Cook until eggs are firm. Season with salt and pepper. Best served on an Italian crusty bun with grated Parmesan cheese and hot red pepper flakes (optional).

With a silly grin on my face, I start pointing: crusty rolls, focaccia, mortadella, soppressata, sausage, bocconcini, dried black olives, watermelon, and chilled white wine.

It's like Christmas morning! We buy cold drinks, paper plates, and more plastic cups. He gives us napkins and plastic utensils. He uncorks the wine. Again, I worry. I ask Agostino if we can drink wine in a public place. He laughs. "In America, no. In Italy, sì."

My heart is singing ... in Italian, of course. Away we go, laden with white plastic grocery bags stretched with food.

> **I ask Agostino if we can drink wine in a public place.**

Sorrido e con una smorfia di sufficienza rispondo cominciando a elencare: panini croccanti, focaccia, mortadella, soppressata, salsiccia, bocconcini, olive nere appassite, cocomero, vino bianco fresco.

Sembra la mattina di ferragosto! Noi prendiamo bibite, piatti di carta e altri bicchieri di carta. Lui ci porge tovaglioli di carta e posate di plastica. Stappa il vino. Ancora una volta qualcosa che non quadra. Chiedo ad Agostino se si possono servire alcolici in un luogo pubblico. Ride. "In America, no. In Italia, sì."

Il cuore gongola ... in italiano, naturalmente. Carichi di buste di plastica bianche stracolme di cibarie, usciamo dal negozio.

We drive to the little park at Villa Comunale. There are trees. There is grass. There are benches and play equipment. It doesn't matter that the grounds are neglected and that the vegetation is scorched by the unforgiving sun. It doesn't matter that graffiti decorates the surrounding walls. It doesn't matter that the play equipment is old and broken. For a moment in time, this moment in time, it is perfect. To us, the grass is lush and green, the gardens are manicured, the play equipment is new, and the breeze is cool.

Randy, every bit the romantic that I am, looks around and says that maybe today will mark the beginning of a new life for the park. Maybe our positive energy will encourage others to return to this place, care for it, and enjoy it. I smile at the thought of an Italian renaissance of picnics.

"We hope that, when the insects take over the world, they will remember with gratitude how we took them along on all our picnics."
– Bill Vaughan, author

Ci dirigiamo in macchina verso il piccolo parco della Villa Comunale. Ci sono gli alberi. C'è l'erba. Ci sono delle panchine e alcuni giochi per bambini. Non importa che il luogo sia tenuto male e che l'erba sia bruciata dal sole. Non importa che il muro di cinta sia imbrattato da una serie di scritte. Non importa che i giochi siano vecchi e rotti. Per una volta nella vita, questa volta, tutto è perfetto. Per noi, l'erba è verde e rigogliosa, il giardino è curatissimo, i giochi sono nuovi e il venticello è piacevolmente fresco.

Randy, romantico tanto quanto me, si guarda intorno e dice che forse oggi sarà l'inizio di una nuova vita per il parco. Forse la nostra energia positiva incoraggerà gli altri a ritornare in questo luogo, a rimetterlo a posto e a goderselo. Mi fa sorridere l'idea che in Italia si possa tornare a fare il picnic.

Perhaps this picnic – and every picnic – is a reminder of things we too often neglect but desperately need in our lives: friends, family, play, and peace. There will always be excuses not to celebrate what's important in life. No grass. No shade. No time. No provisions. No point. It is our job to rise above these excuses.

I sip the cool, crisp white wine. It is delicious, just like the freshly sliced meats and cheeses, and freshly baked bread. The watermelon is a wonder: it has seeds in it! At home, I always buy seedless. Here, I rediscover that spitting out the seeds is half the fun of eating watermelon. I watch as an ant carries a piece of crust across the blanket. How long has it been since that ant enjoyed a picnic? Too long, I am sure. The food, the laughter, the joy – everything about this picnic is real. Everything is perfect.

Forse questo picnic – e ogni picnic – è un modo per richiamare le cose che troppo spesso trascuriamo, ma di cui abbiamo tremendamente bisogno nella nostra vita: la famiglia, gli amici, i giochi e la pace. Ci saranno sempre delle scuse per non festeggiare ciò che è importante nella vita. Non c'è l'erba. Non c'è l'ombra. Non c'è tempo. Non c'è nulla da mangiare. Non c'è nemmeno il posto. Noi queste sono solo delle banali scuse che non ci impediranno di realizzare i nostri desideri.

Sorseggio il vino bianco fresco e frizzante. È semplicemente delizioso, e squisiti sono gli affettati e i formaggi appena tagliati e il pane appena sfornato. Il cocomero è dolcissimo, e ha pure i semi! In Canada compro sempre quello senza semi. Qui riscopro che sputare i semi è la metà del divertimento quando si mangia il cocomero. Osservo una formica che trascina una briciola di pane sulla coperta. Da quanto tempo quella formica non prova il piacere di un picnic? Troppo, ne sono certa. Il cibo, le risate, la gioia: tutto di questo picnic è reale. Tutto è perfetto.

...spitting out the seeds is half the fun of eating watermelon

In this perfectly imperfect world, it's up to each of us to create: **Happiness** where there is sorrow. **Memories** to bring lasting joy. **Innocence** in the face of depravity. **Love** that truly conquers all. **Simplicity** where there is clutter. **Friendship** at every turn. **Patriotism** instead of apathy. **Adventure** over predictability. **Family** to give us roots. **Perfection** we can call our own.

Opposite page:
"Via Custova and My Scooter"
by Anne Parker

"You know what I mean. People are more at ease – a couple of days' sunshine and we become Italians."

– *ATONEMENT*, Ian McEwan

In questo mondo perfettamente imperfetto, sta a ciascuno di noi vedere la felicità laddove alberga il dolore; trasformare i ricordi in una gioia perenne; scorgere l'innocenza nella depravazione; vedere l'amore trionfare su tutto, la semplicità laddove regna il disordine, l'amicizia ad ogni angolo, l'amor di patria invece dell'indifferenza; prendere rischi e non fare solo tutto ciò che è scontato. La famiglia ci dà le radici, la perfezione la creiamo noi.

Life is a picnic.
La vita è un picnic.

Mangia!

This book would not have been possible without the incredible support of so many people. It is with deep gratitude that I acknowledge the following contributors: Jane McDonald, Robert Angle, Monica Hill, Dania Sheldon, Susie Petersiel Berg, Massimo Capra, Farida Zaman, Anne Parker, Sabine Bongartz, Jane D'Alessandro, James D'Alessandro, Cam Robinson, Michelle D'Alessandro-Hatt, Lily Frutti, Joanne Clune, Agostino Laviola, Rocco Nicodemo, Santino Bifulco, and Donna Powell. Thank you for your generosity of spirit, for the trust you placed in me, and for the invaluable role you played in creating this book about picnics.

A very special thank you also goes to my husband, Randy, and my two children, Mason and Kinsey. Thank you for allowing me to share our life, our love, and our picnics. Thank you for your patience and understanding as I created this labour of love, sweat, and years.

The work is done. It's time to relax and have a picnic!

Questo libro non sarebbe stato possibile senza l'incredibile contributo di così tante persone. Sono profondamente grata e riconoscente a Jane McDonald, Robert Angle, Monica Hill, Dania Sheldon, Susie Petersiel Berg, Massimo Capra, Farida Zaman, Anne Parker, Sabine Bongartz, Jane D'Alessandro, James D'Alessandro, Cam Robinson, Michelle D'Alessandro-Hatt, Lily Frutti, Joanne Clune, Agostino Laviola, Rocco Nicodemo, Santino Bifulco e Donna Powell per avermi così generosamente e tenacemente sostenuto, per avermi espresso la loro fiducia e per aver avuto un ruolo così prezioso nella stesura di questo libro sui picnic.

Un ringraziamento speciale a mio marito Randy e ai miei due figli Mason e Kinsey per avermi permesso di condividere la nostra vita, il nostro amore e i nostri picnic e per avermi mostrato tutta la loro pazienza e comprensione nel periodo in cui ho lavorato a quest'opera, che è il frutto dell'amore, del sudore e di anni di duro lavoro.

Ora che è il libro è finito, è il momento di rilassarci e di fare un picnic!

Credits

10   Excerpt from *The Adventures of Huckleberry Finn* by Mark Twain, first published in 1884.

15   Text and Illustration from *THE BEARS' PICNIC* by Stan Berenstain and Jan Berenstain, copyright ©1966 by Berenstain Enterprises, Inc. Used by permission of Random House Children's Books, a division of Random House, Inc.

Text and Illustration from *THE BEARS' PICNIC* reprinted by permission of SLL/Sterling Lord Literistic, Inc. Copyright 1966 by Stanley and Janice Berenstain.

17   Excerpt reprinted with permission from *The Food Encyclopedia*, published by Robert Rose Inc., 2006.

18   Excerpt from *Anne of Green Gables* reprinted with permission. Anne of Green Gables, characters, names and related indicia are trademarks and Canadian official marks of the Anne of Green Gables Licensing Authority Inc. L.M. Montgomery is a trademark of Heirs of L.M. Montgomery Inc.

19   Excerpt from *English Picnics* by Georgina Battiscombe, The Country Book Club edition, published in 1951.

21   One Illustration and Text, p. 60 from *THE NEW WE COME AND GO*. Copyright 1956 by Scott, Foresman and Company. Reprinted by permission of Pearson Education, Inc.

22   Excerpt from "The Art of Picnicking" in *The Armchair James Beard*, by James Beard, edited by John Ferrone (2004). By permission of The Blumer Literary Agency.

25   Excerpt from the moral to "Little Red Riding Hood," *Perrault's Fairy Tales* by Charles Perrault, 1697. Translated by A.E. Johnson; translation of verse morals by S.R. Littlewood, 1912 Wordsworth Editions, Dover Publications, 2004.

27   Excerpt and Still from *Written on the Wind*. Courtesy of Universal Studios Licensing LLLP. Third-party consent from CMG Worldwide.

28   Excerpt from *The Devil's Picnic* by Taras Grescoe, first published by Bloomsbury Publishing, 2005.

29   Recipe courtesy of Egg Farmers of Canada. Used with permission. www.eggs.ca

31   Excerpt from *Romeo and Juliet* by William Shakespeare.

34	Lyric Excerpt from "Picnic." Written by George Duning and Steve Allen. Used by Permission of Canadian Shapiro Bernstein o/b/o Shapiro, Bernstein & Co., Inc. – Film Division. All Rights Reserved. International Copyright Secured.
37	Excerpt and Still from *THE YOGI BEAR SHOW*™ & © Hanna-Barbera. Courtesy of Warner Bros. Entertainment Inc. Used with permission.
38	Excerpt and Recipe from *Aunt Maud's Recipe Book from the kitchen of L.M. Montgomery* by Elaine Crawford & Kelly Crawford. Copyright © 1996. Used with permission.
39	Artwork and Caption attributed to Sultan Muhammad. *Lovers' Picnic*, painting (recto), text (verso), folio from a manuscript of the Divan (Collected Works) of Hafiz, c. 1526-27. Ink, opaque watercolor, and gold on paper: 19 x 12.4 cm (7 1/2 x 4 7/8 in.). Harvard Art Museums, Arthur M. Sackler Museum, Gift of Stuart Cary Welch in honor of Edith Iselin Gilbert Welch, 2007.183. Photo: Katya Kallsen © President and Fellows of Harvard College. Inscription written by Hafiz; translated by Martin Bernard Dickson. Courtesy of *Harvard Magazine*.
41	Excerpt and Cover Image from *Good Wood News* (Vol. 3, No. 6, July/August 1987), Lansing Buildall. Used with permission. Courtesy of RONA.
42	Image from *Abbey's Own*, April 11, 1987. Used with permission. Courtesy of *North Oakville Today*.
43	Recipe courtesy of Ontario Greenhouse Vegetable Growers. Used with permission. www.ontariogreenhouse.com
44	Excerpt reprinted with the permission of Scribner, a Division of Simon & Schuster, Inc., from ROADSIDE PICNIC by Arkady and Boris Strugatsky, translated by Antonina W. Bouis. Copyright © 1977 by Macmillan Publishing Co., Inc. All rights reserved.
44	Excerpt from *Little Women* by Louisa May Alcott, first published in 1868.
44	Cartoon from www.CartoonStock.com. Used with permission.
46	Final sentence from speech: Lester B. Pearson's Address on the inauguration of the national flag of Canada on February 15, 1965. Source: Library and Archives Canada/ Lester B. Pearson fonds.
47	Jann Arden, singer, songwriter, and author, as quoted in Canadian Health & Lifestyle/Winter 2005/www.healthandlifestyle.ca. Used with permission.

48   Cartoon © Henry Martin/The New Yorker Collection/www.cartoonbank.com. Used with permission.

48   Jon Montgomery, Olympic gold medalist, as quoted in Canadian Health & Lifestyle/Summer 2010/www.healthandlifestyle.ca. Used with permission.

49   Canada Day Picnic Sandwich Recipe by The Canadian Living Magazine Test Kitchen. © Canadian Living. Used with permission.

50   Statement by the Prime Minister of Canada 2010 http://www.pm.gc.ca/eng/media.asp?id=3118 Reproduced with the permission of the Minister of Public Works and Government Services, 2010, and Courtesy of the Privy Council Office.

51   Excerpt from *Simple Abundance, A Daybook of Comfort and Joy* by Sarah Ban Breathnach. Copyright 1995. All rights reserved. Used with permission.

53   Lyrics from THE TEDDY BEARS' PICNIC. Words by Jimmy Kennedy. Music by John W. Bratton © 1947 (Renewed) WB Music Corp. and EMI Music Publishing Ltd. All Rights Administered by WB Music Corp. All Rights Reserved. Used by Permission of Alfred Publishing Co., Inc.

        Teddy Bears' Picnic – J. Kennedy/J. Bratton. © 1947 M. Witmark & Sons, B. Feldman & Co. Ltd. Used by permission of EMI Allans Music Australia Pty Limited (ABN 30 004 057 541) P.O. Box 35, Pyrmont, NSW 2009, Australia. International copyright secured. All rights reserved.

54   Excerpt from Henry David Thoreau's journal, April 24, 1859.

55   Still from the Film *Picnic*, © 1955, renewed 1983 Columbia Pictures Industries, Inc. All Rights Reserved. Used with permission of MPTVIMAGES.COM.

55   Excerpt from the play *Picnic* by William Inge. © 1953, 1955, William Inge. Renewed 1981, 1983, Helene Connell. All Rights Reserved. Used with permission of Random House, Inc., New York, NY.

        Excerpt from the play *Picnic* by William Inge. Reprinted by permission of International Creative Management, Inc. Copyright © 1953 by William Inge.

57	Excerpt and Illustration reprinted with the permission of Atheneum Books for Young Readers, an imprint of Simon & Schuster Children's Publishing Division from THE WIND IN THE WILLOWS by Kenneth Grahame, illustrated by Ernest H. Shepard. Copyright 1933, 1953 Charles Scribner's Sons; copyrights renewed © 1961 Ernest H. Shepard and © 1981 Charles Scribner's Sons and Mary Eleanor Jessie Knox. Illustration reprinted with the permission of Curtis Brown. Copyright © The Estate of E.H. Shepard and Egmont Books Ltd. Illustration provided by Egmont UK Ltd London and printed with permission.
59	Excerpt and Illustration from THE HOUSE AT POOH CORNER by A.A. Milne, illustrated by E.H. Shepard, copyright 1928 by E.P. Dutton, renewed © 1956 by A.A. Milne. Used by permission of Dutton Children's Books, A Division of Penguin Young Readers Group, A Member of Penguin Group (USA) Inc., 245 Hudson Street, New York, NY 10014. All rights reserved. From *The House at Pooh Corner* by A.A. Milne. Text copyright © The Trustees of the Pooh Properties 1928. Published by Egmont UK Ltd London and used with permission. Illustration from THE HOUSE AT POOH CORNER by A.A. Milne, illustrated by E.H. Shepard. Copyright © The Estate of E.H. Shepard and Egmont Books Ltd. Used with permission. Illustration provided by Egmont UK Ltd London and printed with permission.
63	Excerpt and Illustration from Lezlie Evans *The Bunnies' Picnic* © 2007 by Lezlie Evans, Illustrated by Kay Chorao. Reprinted by Permission of Disney•Hyperion, an imprint of Disney Book Group LLC. All Rights Reserved.
66	Excerpt from *Alla ricerca di Rocco e i suoi fratelli: la Basilicata di Luchino Visconti* by Teresa Megale, as quoted in Pisticci Tourism Map/Brochure, Amministrazione Comunale. Used with permission.
68	Excerpt from *Cristo si è fermato ad Eboli* by Carlo Levi, as quoted in Pisticci Tourism Map/Brochure, Amministrazione Comunale. Used with permission.
76	Excerpt from *Food for Friends: Simply Delicious Menus for Easy Entertaining* by Fran Warde. Text © Fran Warde 2002. First published in the United States in 2002 by Ryland Peters & Small, Inc., New York, NY. Used with permission.

92 Excerpted from *Atonement* by Ian McEwan. Copyright © 2001 Ian McEwan. Reprinted by permission of Knopf Canada.

Excerpt from *Atonement* by Ian McEwan, published by Jonathan Cape. Reprinted by permission of The Random House Group Ltd.

Copyright © 2001 Ian McEwan. Reproduced by permission of the author c/o Rogers, Coleridge & White Ltd., 20 Powis Mews, London W11 1JN.

Excerpt from ATONEMENT by Ian McEwan, copyright © 2002 by Ian McEwan. Used by permission of Doubleday, a division of Random House, Inc.

The life of a man doesn't end when he dies. The life of a man lives on as long as the memory lives.

La vita di un uomo non finisce con la morte, ma egli continuerà a vivere fino a quando sarà vivo il suo ricordo.

– *Agostino Laviola, Pisticci taxi driver, July 21, 2008*

www.lifeisapicnic.ca